MICHAEL FOX

Techniques

of

Critical

Reasoning

D1563611

Techniques

of

Critical

Reasoning

David B. Annis

Ball State University

CHARLES E. MERRILL PUBLISHING COMPANY
A Bell & Howell Company
Columbus, Ohio

Published by
Charles E. Merrill Publishing Company
A Bell & Howell Company
Columbus, Ohio 43216

ISBN: 0-675-08906-9

Library of Congress Catalog Card Number: 73-81554

1 2 3 4 5 6 7 — 80 79 78 77 76 75 74

Printed in the United States of America

To Linda and Tek

Preface

This book is designed to provide the reader with a working knowledge of some of the basic techniques of critical reasoning. Frequently a student has difficulty in thinking critically about an issue. He may not be able to formulate the problem in a precise way, or he may not be able to construct or evaluate arguments in support of some thesis. This book is intended to be of use to such a student.

Chapter 1 is a general introduction to logic and stresses putting arguments into standard form. Techniques for proving the deductive validity or invalidity of arguments are presented in the second chapter. Several valid argument forms are discussed and others may be added by the instructor. Some of the more frequent types of inductive arguments, as well as common fallacies, are presented in the next chapter. The first three chapters should thus provide the reader with an understanding of some of the basic concepts of deductive and inductive logic. This understanding will aid the reader in constructing and evaluating arguments.

When attempting to think critically about an issue, imprecision frequently causes difficulties. Chapter 4 contains a discussion of several features of language that produce imprecision and techniques for avoiding this problem. This chapter should thus aid the student in formulating issues and arguments in a more precise way.

The last chapter extends the techniques of the first four chapters to argumentative essays. An interesting essay on civil disobedience by Rudolph H. Weingartner is reprinted and critically discussed. Since this chapter requires the student to critically evaluate a longer essay, it is more demanding than the other four chapters. It will thus require more attention.

There are exercises at the end of almost all the sections so the reader can test whether he understands the material and can apply it to concrete examples. Answers are provided to most of the odd-numbered problems. An attempt has been made to make the examples interesting.

I wish to thank my wife Linda for all her help. She provided most of the examples for chapter 3, helped me to clarify a number of passages in the book, and did all the typing. I also would like to thank Rudolph H. Weingartner for allowing me to reprint his essay on civil disobedience.

Contents

1

The Nature of Logic

1-1   Arguments

In order to support a statement we often give an argument. To support the claim that any modern war is morally wrong, Jones might argue that it is wrong to kill innocent people. But any modern war involves killing a great many innocent people. Therefore any modern war is wrong. Now is this a good argument? The study of logic will help to answer this question.

Logic deals with the conditions under which arguments are logically correct. As the term will be used, an *argument* consists of one or more statements, called the *premises,* which are given in support of another statement, called the *conclusion.* For our purposes a statement is simply a declarative sentence. In the above argument the conclusion is that any modern war is morally wrong. The premises consist of the statements that it is wrong to kill innocent people and that any modern war involves killing a great many innocent people. A uniform way of stating an argument is to list each premise separately, draw a line under them, and write the conclusion under the line. The statements in the argument are numbered consecutively, and the symbol ∴ which stands for the word "therefore" is written to the left of the numbered conclusion. When an argument is stated in this way it is in *standard form.* If we put Jones's argument into standard form, it would be:

(1)   It is wrong to kill innocent people.
(2)   Any modern war involves killing a great
        many innocent people.

∴ (3)   Any modern war is morally wrong.

Putting an argument into standard form makes it easier to evaluate. To put an argument into this form we must of course be able to identify the premises and the conclusion of the argument. This is not always easy. Frequently the conclusion is stated first and then the premises are given. At other times the conclusion comes last. Sometimes the conclusion is wedged in between premises. To help identify the conclusion, ask the question, "What is the main point that is being argued for?" There are also some linguistic clues. "Therefore," "thus," "hence," "so," "consequently," and "it follows that" are expressions that frequently precede the conclusion. To help identify the premises, ask the question, "What statements are given in support of the conclusion?" Again there are some linguistic clues. "For," "since," and "because" are expressions that frequently precede premises.

Quite often an argument for some conclusion will contain subsidiary arguments. These arguments are usually intended to support various statements that then are used as premises for the main conclusion. To put such an argument into standard form requires one to identify the main conclusion, the premises in support of this conclusion, and the arguments supporting these premises.

Some examples will illustrate how to put arguments into standard form. Take the following argument:

> It is wrong to inflict suffering on another person. Thus
> punishment cannot be justified since that is exactly what
> we do when we punish a person.

In this example the word "thus" indicates what the conclusion is. The first sentence in the argument is a premise. The second premise follows the word "since." In standard form the argument is:

(1)   It is wrong to inflict suffering on another
        person.

    (2)   That is exactly what we do when we punish a person.

∴ (3)   Punishment cannot be justified.

Premise (2) is not as precise as it might be. Frequently when an argument is put into standard form the premises or conclusion may need to be rewritten in order to make the argument more precise. We have to be careful when we do this since we do not want to distort the original argument. To make premise (2) more precise, the argument can be expressed as:

    (1)   It is wrong to inflict suffering on another person.
    (2)   When we punish a person we inflict suffering on him.

∴ (3)   Punishment cannot be justified.

Next consider this argument:

It is clear that prison reform is essential. Statistics show that a large percentage of the prisoners that are released violate the law again and are returned to prison. So being in prison does not rehabilitate a person. But that is one of the main purposes of prisons.

The main point of the argument is that prison reform is essential. If we put the argument into standard form it would be:

    (1)   Statistics show that a large percentage of the prisoners that are released violate the law again and are returned to prison.
∴ (2)   Being in prison does not rehabilitate a person.
    (3)   One of the main purposes of prisons is the rehabilitation of prisoners.

∴ (4)   It is clear that prison reform is essential.

Premise (1) is offered in support of (2); (2) and (3) are then given as support for (4). Notice that the third premise has been re-phrased to make the argument more precise.

A slightly more complex example is:

> In a free society all those people whose lives are greatly affected by a social institution have a right to participate in the formulation of the policies of that institution. Thus students here in the United States have the right to partici-pate in the formulation of the policies of universities. After all, their lives are greatly affected by the university since it affects their outlook on life, their job opportuni-ties, and the quality of their lives in general. So certainly students' lives are greatly affected. Furthermore the Unit-ed States is a free society and universities are social institu-tions. But are students participating in the universities? No![1]

The main point of the argument is that students here in the United States have the right to participate in the formulation of the policies of the universities. This conclusion is supported by the assertion that in a free society all those people whose lives are greatly affected by a social institution have a right to participate in the formulation of the policies of that institution. It then is argued that students' lives are greatly affected by the university. The subsidiary argument for this statement consists of the premise that the university affects their outlook on life, their job opportunities, and the quality of their lives in general. It also is claimed that the United States is a free society and universities are social institu-tions. The argument in standard form is:

(1)   In a free society all those people whose lives are greatly affected by a social institution have a right to participate in the formula-tion of the policies of that institution.

(2)   The university affects students' outlook on life, their job opportunities, and the quality of their lives in general.

---

1. This argument is a paraphrase of one to be found in Earl J. McGrath's *Should Students Share the Power?* (Philadelphia: Temple University Press, 1970), pp. 70-71.

∴ (3) Students' lives are greatly affected by the
university.

(4) The United States is a free society and universities are social institutions.

∴ (5) Students here in the United States have the
right to participate in the formulation of the
policies of the universities.

Quite often when we give an argument for some conclusion we
do not state all the premises. Some of the premises may simply be
assumed and not be made explicit in the argument. Smith might
argue that Jones will not win the election since his district is
Democratic. In standard form his argument would be:

(1) Jones's district is Democratic.

∴ (2) Jones will not win the election.

One unstated premise that Smith might be assuming is that Jones
is not a Democrat. The argument can now be expressed as:

(1) Jones's district is Democratic.
(2) Jones is not a Democrat.

∴ (3) Jones will not win the election.

Here an assumed premise has been made explicit. Smith might also
be assuming that any person who is not a Democrat in a Democratic district cannot win an election. Thus in more complete form
Smith's argument is:

(1) Jones's district is Democratic.
(2) Jones is not a Democrat.
(3) Any person who is not a Democrat in a
Democratic district cannot win an election.

∴ (4) Jones will not win the election.

In the original argument (2) and (3) were both unstated premises;
they have now been made explicit.

An argument for some conclusion may seem persuasive until an unstated premise is made explicit. Premises (1) and (2) of Smith's argument may be obviously true so we may be persuaded to accept the conclusion. However, when the assumed premise (3) is made explicit, we may have some doubts about the argument. Making explicit unstated premises is thus helpful when critically evaluating an argument. When putting an argument into standard form we should thus try to make explicit any unstated premises.

Making assumed premises explicit is frequently a difficult task. If Smith argues that Jones will not win the election since his district is Democratic, he *may* be assuming that Jones is not a Democrat and any person who is not a Democrat in a Democratic district cannot win an election. But he also may be making completely different assumptions. Perhaps his reasoning is this: Jones's district is Democratic and since Jones is a Democrat and has criticized the Democrats so severely, he will not win the election. In standard form his argument would be:

> (1) Jones's district is Democratic.
> (2) Jones is a Democrat and his criticized the Democrats severely.
> _____
> ∴ (3) Jones will not win the election.

Or maybe Smith's reasoning is:

> (1) Jones's district is Democratic.
> (2) People who are Democratic in Jones's district will not vote for Jones.
> _____
> ∴ (3) Jones will not win the election.

If we are just given the premise that Jones's district is Democratic and the conclusion that he will not win the election, we cannot determine what extra premises are being assumed and left unstated. In this case we simply have to ask Smith what he is taking for granted. If we cannot ask him, we cannot determine what his argument is.

Sometimes it is possible to determine the unstated premises of an argument by appealing to background information that we have. Suppose it is argued that Smith deserves to be punished for he intentionally killed an innocent child. Since it is commonly believed that people who intentionally kill innocent children deserve to be punished, it would be likely that this was an assumed premise in the argument. Making it explicit gives us:

(1) Smith intentionally killed an innocent child.
(2) People who intentionally kill innocent children deserve to be punished.

∴ (3) Smith deserves to be punished.

Exercises

A. Put the following arguments into standard form. For these arguments you do not have to add any unstated premises.

1. Wars invariably have resulted in more evil than good. The conflict in Southeast Asia is certainly a war, so it too will probably result in more evil than good.

2. It is unjust not to punish violators of the law, for it is unjust to treat a person in a way that he does not deserve to be treated; and if a person violates the law, he deserves to be punished.

3. Sometimes our senses deceive us. But if they do, then they might be deceiving us right now (e.g., we might be having a very coherent hallucination). If so, then we do not know that they are not deceiving us now. Consequently, for all we know our senses are deceiving us now. It follows that we cannot rely on our senses.

4. If we are just, we recognize the equal intrinsic value of every person. Now to do this is to treat each person so as to provide equal opportunity for that person. So we certainly are not just, since we have failed to do this. We just have not provided equal opportunity for all.

5. If the majority rules the government, minority rights are not assured. But if minority rights are not assured, the government is not just. On the other hand if the minority rules, then it is not fair to the majority. But if it is not fair to the majority, then again the government is not just. Thus in a democracy you cannot have justice since either the majority rules or the minority does.

6. I think the course will be a good one. When Jones teaches it the course is good. Jones and Smith both have good personalities, approach the course in the same way, enjoy students, and are good teachers. Since they are both so similar, Smith's course surely will be good.

7. Most students on this campus do not feel that the university has any right to regulate their private lives. This is clear from a recent survey where 90 percent of those polled responded that the university did not have such a right. But if the majority of students at this campus feel that way, most students at other campuses probably feel the same way. Most students then are fed up with being treated like children.

8. There has to be more than one ethical standard since many different groups of people have conflicting moral judgments. It is rather obvious that if different groups of people disagree in their moral judgments, there are going to be different standards. Other nations accept polygamy. We think this is wrong so there must be different standards.

9. It is questionable whether this country is a democracy for if a country is a democracy the power lies in the hands of the people. That is what a democracy is. But if the power lies in the hands of the people, it follows that when the majority of those people are opposed to a course of action that action will not be pursued by the country. Thus if a course of action is followed by a country when the majority of the people are opposed to it, that country is not a democracy. Now look at our country. Have not various actions been pursued when the majority of people have been opposed?

B. Put these arguments into standard form also. Make explicit premises that seem to be assumed. Remember that sometimes it is difficult if not impossible to determine what premises are being left unstated.

1. An act of racial discrimination is wrong since it involves treating a person unfairly.

2. In order to know that some statement is true, we have to be absolutely certain that the statement is true. Hence we do not know that any statements are true.

3. A social institution is racist if it intentionally discriminates against individuals on the basis of race. Hence University A is racist.

4. Intentionally discriminating against a person is worse than unintentionally discriminating against a person. So what Jones did is worse than what Smith did.

5. If viability determines whether the fetus is a human being and viability depends on the relative state of technology, then whether the fetus is human depends on the relative state of technology. Thus viability does not determine whether the fetus is a human being.

Answers to Selected Exercises

A.

1. (1) Wars invariably have resulted in more evil than good.
    (2) The conflict in Southeast Asia is certainly a war.

    ∴ (3) The war in Southeast Asia will probably result in more evil than good.

Notice that the conclusion has been rephrased to make it more precise.

3. (1) Sometimes our senses deceive us.
    (2) If our senses deceive us sometimes, then our senses might be deceiving us right now (e.g., we might be having a very coherent hallucination).
    (3) If our senses might be deceiving us right now (e.g., we might be having a very coherent hallucination), then we do not know that our senses are not deceiving us now.
    ∴ (4) For all we know our senses are deceiving us now.

    ∴ (5) We cannot rely on our senses.

The second and third sentences of the argument have been rewritten to make the argument more precise.

5.   (1) If the majority rules the government, minority rights are not assured.

           (2) If minority rights are not assured, the government is not just.

           (3) If the minority rules, then it is not fair to the majority.

           (4) If it is not fair to the majority, then the government is not just.

           (5) In a democracy either the majority rules the government or the minority does.

∴ (6) In a democracy you cannot have justice.

7.   (1) Ninety percent of the students polled at this university responded that the university did not have any right to regulate their private lives.

∴ (2) Most of the students on this campus do not feel that the university has any right to regulate their private lives.

           (3) If the majority of students at this campus feel this way, then most students at other campuses probably feel the same way.

∴ (4) Most students are fed up with being treated like children.

9.   (1) If a country is a democracy, the power lies in the hands of the people.

           (2) If the power lies in the hands of the people, it follows that when the majority of these people are opposed to a course of action that action will not be pursued by the country.

∴ (3) If a course of action is followed by a country when the majority of the people are opposed to it, then that country is not a democracy.

Essentially this is the argument. On the basis of this argument the question is raised whether our form of government is really democratic. If the last sentence of the exercise were turned into a premise, the conclusion would be that our form of government is not democratic.

B. These are *some* of the ways the arguments might be formulated. There are other ways too.

1. (1) An act of racial discrimination involves treating a person unfairly.
    (2) Acts of treating a person unfairly are wrong.

    ∴ (3) An act of racial discrimination is wrong.

3. (1) A social institution is racist if it intentionally discriminates against individuals on the basis of race.
    (2) University A is a social institution.
    (3) It intentionally discriminates against individuals on the basis of race.

    ∴ (4) University A is racist.

5. (1) If viability determines whether the fetus is a human being and viability depends on the relative state of technology, then whether the fetus is a human being depends on the relative state of technology.
    (2) Whether the fetus is a human being does not depend on the relative state of technology.
    (3) Viability depends on the relative state of technology.

    ∴ (4) Viability does not determine whether the fetus is a human being.

1-2   Truth and Logical Correctness

One way to criticize an argument is to argue that one or more of
the premises is false. Suppose someone were to argue that justice
cannot be achieved in a democracy since minority rights cannot be
assured in a democracy, and if they cannot be, then justice cannot
be achieved. In standard form this argument is:

> (1) Minority rights cannot be assured in a
>   democracy.
> (2) If minority rights cannot be assured in a
>   democracy, then justice cannot be achieved
>   in a democracy.
> _____
> ∴ (3) Justice cannot be achieved in a democracy.

To criticize this argument we might argue that premise (1) is false.
But there are other ways to criticize an argument besides arguing
that one or more of the premises is false. Imagine that someone
argued that most people in the United States are opposed to
welfare spending since a random sample of wealthy Republicans
showed that most members of the sample were opposed to such
spending. In standard form this argument is:

> (1) A random sample of wealthy Republicans
>   showed that most members of the sample
>   were opposed to welfare spending.
> _____
> ∴ (2) Most people in the United States are op-
>   posed to welfare spending.

Assuming premise (1) to be true, we can still criticize the argument.
The premise of this argument does not adequately support the
conclusion. There are then at least two very important ways to
criticize an argument. We can argue that one or more of the
premises is false, or we can argue that even if the premises are all
true, they do not adequately support the conclusion.

The second type of criticism has to do with the logical relation
between a set of premises and a conclusion. It is this relation with
which logicians are primarily concerned. An argument is said to be
logically correct just in case the premises provide adequate support

for the conclusion. If an argument is not logically correct, then it is *fallacious.*

Logical correctness and truth must be carefully distinguished. Statements are true or false; arguments are logically correct or incorrect. Whether a set of premises adequately supports a conclusion is independent of whether the premises are in fact true or false. All the premises of an argument may be true and yet those premises still might not support the conclusion. Here is such an example:

>   (1) John Kennedy was president of the United States.
>   (2) Lyndon Johnson was president of the United States.
> _____
>
> ∴ (3) Richard Nixon was president of the United States.

On the other hand, all or some of the premises of an argument may be false and yet those premises might adequately support its conclusion. Here are two such examples:

>   (1) No women have ever been discriminated against.
>   (2) If no women have ever been discriminated against, then all women are happy.
> _____
>
> ∴ (3) All women are happy.

>   (1) Einstein was a great physicist.
>   (2) All great physicists were Italian.
> _____
>
> ∴ (3) Einstein was Italian.

In the first argument, premises (1) and (2) are false. Even though they are false, the premises still provide adequate support for the conclusion. In the second argument, premise (1) is true while (2) is false. Again the premises adequately support the conclusion. An argument that is both logically correct and has true premises is said to be *sound.* Thus the following argument is sound:

(1)   All men are mortal.
(2)   Socrates was a man.

∴ (3)   Socrates was mortal.

1-3   Deductive and Inductive Logic

There are basically two main areas in logic: deductive and inductive logic. The former deals with the conditions under which an argument is *deductively valid* while the latter deals with the conditions under which an argument is *inductively strong.* An argument is logically correct if it is either deductively valid or inductively strong.

The essential difference between a deductively valid argument and one that is inductively strong is as follows. If an argument is deductively valid and it has true premises, then the conclusion *must* be true. A deductively valid argument cannot have true premises and a false conclusion. Inductively strong arguments lack this feature. It is possible for such an argument to have true premises and a false conclusion. However, if an argument is inductively strong and has true premises, then the conclusion is *probably* true. A deductively valid argument with true premises conclusively establishes the conclusion, while an inductively strong argument with true premises makes the conclusion probable but does not conclusively prove it. Even though such an argument does not prove the conclusion, it does provide adequate support for the conclusion.

The following two arguments are deductively valid.

(1)   All men are mortal.
(2)   Socrates was a man.

∴ (3)   Socrates was mortal.

(1)   If God exists, there would be no evil.
(2)   There is evil.

∴ (3)   God does not exist.

If the premises of these two arguments were true, then the

conclusions also would have to be true. The next two arguments are not deductively valid but are inductively strong.

> (1) No man has ever run the mile in less than two minutes.
> (2) Jones is a man.

> ∴ (3) Jones will not run the mile in less than two minutes.

> (1) A random sample of 1,000 students at a university with a total student population of 5,000 yielded the result that 98 percent of the students favored legalizing abortion.

> ∴ (2) Most students at the university favor legalizing abortion.

If the premises of these arguments were true, it would still be possible for the conclusions to be false. Nevertheless the premises make the conclusions probable.

Exercises

Which of the following arguments are deductively valid, inductively strong, or neither?

1.
> (1) Two of the professors from New York that I had were hard graders.
> (2) The professor from New York that Jones had was a hard grader.

> ∴ (3) Most professors from New York must be hard graders.

2.
> (1) If all men are equal, then each man should be treated equally.
> (2) All men are equal.

> ∴ (3) Each man should be treated equally.

3.
> (1) Cars A and B are quite similar in that both

are brand X, model Y, both have eight-cylinder engines with the same cubic capacity, both operate on the same type of carburetion system, and both are in good operating condition.

(2) When car A is driven by Jones, it gets fifteen miles per gallon of gas.

∴ (3) If car B is driven by Jones, it will probably get approximately fifteen miles per gallon of gas.

4.   (1) If every event has a cause, then our actions are causally determined.

(2) If our actions are causally determined, then our actions are not free.

(3) If our actions are not free, then we are not responsible for our actions.

∴ (4) If every event has a cause, we are not responsible for our actions.

5.   (1) Either students will gain equal representation in the governance of the university or the outdated curriculum will continue.

(2) The students did gain equal representation in the governance of the university.

∴ (3) The outdated curriculum will not continue.

Answers to Selected Exercises

1. Neither
3. Inductively strong
5. Neither

1-4   Summary of Basic Concepts

1. *Logic* deals with the conditions under which arguments are logically correct.

2. An *argument* consists of one or more statements, called the

premises, which are given in support of another statement, called the *conclusion.*

3. An argument is in *standard form* if each premise is listed separately, a line is drawn under them, the conclusion is written under the line, each statement in the argument is numbered consecutively, and the symbol ∴ is written to the left of the numbered conclusion.

4. An argument is *logically correct* if the premises provide adequate support for the conclusion. Thus an argument is logically correct if it is deductively valid or inductively strong.

5. An argument is *fallacious* if it is not logically correct.

6. An argument is *sound* if it is logically correct and its premises are all true.

Exercises

Carefully explain your answers and give examples whenever appropriate.

1. Can an argument be logically correct and yet have false premises?

2. If an argument is logically correct does it follow that the conclusion is true?

3. Carefully explain the difference between logical correctness and truth.

4. Can an argument be deductively valid and yet not be sound?

5. Can an argument be sound and yet neither be deductively valid nor inductively strong?

6. Can an argument be sound and yet have a false conclusion?

7. Can an argument have all true premises and a true conclusion and yet be fallacious?

8. If an argument is neither deductively valid nor inductively strong, is it fallacious?

9. What are two important ways to criticize an argument?

10. What is the basic difference between a deductively valid argument and one that is inductively strong?

Deductive Logic

2-1 Deductive Validity

The most important concept in deductive logic is deductive validity. An argument is said to be *deductively valid* just in case it is not possible for the premises to be true and the conclusion false.[1] It follows from this definition of validity that if the premises of a valid argument are true, then the conclusion also must be true.

The concepts of truth and validity must be carefully distinguished. Validity depends solely upon the logical relation that a set of premises bears to a conclusion. Whether an argument is valid is independent of the question of the *actual* truth or falsity of the premises or conclusion. The deductive logician does not ask: Are the premises and conclusion of an argument true? Instead he asks: If the premises are assumed to be true, does it follow that the conclusion also would have to be true? An argument might be valid and yet have some or all false premises and a true or false conclusion. On the other hand an argument might have all true premises and a true conclusion and yet be invalid. The arguments below demonstrate this clearly. "T" and "F" stand for "true" and "false" respectively.

(1)   George Washington was Russian.   F

---

1. For brevity we will often speak of validity instead of deductive validity.

(2)	All Russians are Spanish.	F

∴ (3)	George Washington was Spanish.	F

(1)	George Washington was Russian.	F
(2)	All Russians are male.	F

∴ (3)	George Washington was male.	T

(1)	George Washington was Russian.	F
(2)	All Russians were born on earth.	T

∴ (3)	George Washington was born on earth.	T

(1)	George Washington was an American.	T
(2)	All Americans are Russian.	F

∴ (3)	George Washington was Russian.	F

(1)	George Washington was president.	T
(2)	Abraham Lincoln was president.	T

∴ (3)	John Kennedy was president.	T

The first four arguments are valid. If the premises were true, the conclusions also would have to be true. However, the fifth argument is invalid. The premises do not support the conclusion; they are logically irrelevant to it.

The main reason for being interested in validity is that it is truth preserving. If the premises of an argument are true, then the validity of the argument ensures that the conclusion is also true. Truth is preserved in the conclusion. Hence one way to establish the truth of a statement is to construct a valid argument with true premises that has the statement in question as its conclusion. To take an example, if it could be shown that all wars involve the degradation of human life and that the degradation of human life is always morally wrong, then it would have been conclusively demonstrated that no war is ever morally justified.

Invalidity, however, is not truth preserving. Even though the premises of an argument are true, as long as the argument is invalid, it does not follow that the conclusion also is true. To slightly modify the above example, imagine that an invalid argument is given with the conclusion that some wars are morally justified. Even if the premises of the argument are true, the conclusion has not been shown to be true. Hence one is not rationally compelled to accept the conclusion. It should be noted that if an argument is invalid it does not follow that the conclusion is false. All that follows is that the argument does not prove that the conclusion is true. The conclusion may be true but the argument does not show that it is.

Two questions should be asked if one is concerned with whether an argument conclusively proves that a conclusion is true. First, is the argument valid? If it is invalid, the argument does not prove the conclusion. Second, if the argument is valid, are the premises true? If there is at least one false premise, again the conclusion has not been shown to be true. If all the premises are true and the argument is valid, the conclusion must be true. In this case the argument is sound.

2-2 Logical Form

How do we show that an argument is valid? Consider the following two arguments:

> (1) If women want equal rights, then they must be willing to accept the responsibilities implied by the rights.
> (2) Women want equal rights.

> ∴ (3) They must be willing to accept the responsibilities implied by the rights.

> (1) If our actions are causally determined, then we lack free will.
> (2) Our actions are causally determined.

> ∴ (3) We lack free will.

These two arguments have the same *logical form*. This becomes evident when the statements in the argument are symbolized. Let the capital letter *A* be an abbreviation of the statement "Women want equal rights" and let *B* abbreviate the statement "Women must be willing to accept the responsibilities implied by the rights." In the future to abbreviate statements we shall write:

　A: Women want equal rights.

This indicates that the letter *A* is an abbreviation of the statement "Women want equal rights." Given the above symbolization, the first argument is:

　　(1)　If *A*, then *B*.
　　(2)　*A*.
　　―――――――――――――
　∴ (3)　*B*.

If we let

　C: Our actions are causally determined.
　D: We lack free will.

then the second argument becomes:

　　(1)　If *C*, then *D*.
　　(2)　*C*.
　　―――――――――――――
　∴ (3)　*D*.

Logical form pertains to the structure of the argument and not to its content. Since both of the arguments have the same structure, they have the same logical form.

The reason logical form is important when considering the validity of an argument is that an argument is valid by virtue of its logical form alone. In order to determine whether an argument is valid, all we need to consider is its logical form or structure.

The common structure of the above two arguments can be represented as:

　　(1)　If ***, then _ _ _.
　　(2)　***.
　　―――――――――――――
　∴ (3)　_ _ _.

If statement A is put in place of the asterisks and statement B in place of the dashes, the result is the first argument. If statement C replaces the asterisks and D the dashes, the second argument results. Using asterisks and dashes enables us to represent the logical structure that is common to these two arguments. The only problem with using asterisks and dashes to exhibit the logical structure of arguments is that these symbols are somewhat cumbersome. To exhibit the logical form of an argument we will instead use the lower case letters p, q, r, and so on. Thus the form of the above two arguments is:

> (1) If p, then q.
> (2) p.
> _____
> $\therefore$ (3) q.

The letters p and q are *not* abbreviations of particular statements. They are simply letters in place of which a statement may be written. Thus the schema

> (1) If p, then q.
> (2) p.
> _____
> $\therefore$ (3) q.

is not an argument but an *argument form.* It becomes an argument if we replace the letters p and q by statements. This particular argument form happens to be valid. If an argument form is valid, then any argument that has that form is valid. Thus one way to show that an argument is valid is to show that it has a valid argument form. In the next section several valid elementary argument forms are discussed.

2-3   Some Valid Elementary Argument Forms

Let us define a *simple statement* as a statement that does not contain any other statement as a component. For example "Jones is here," "All men are mortal," and "War is evil" are all simple statements. A *compound statement* is a statement that contains another statement as a component. "Jones is here and Smith is away," "Either war is wrong or it is right," and "If all men are rational, then Socrates is rational" are all compound statements. The components of the first compound statement are "Jones is here" and "Smith is away." The components of the next two compound statements are "War is wrong" and "War is right," and "All men are rational" and "Socrates is rational." There are a number of ways of forming compound statements. We will consider several ways of forming such statements and various valid argument forms that involve these compound statements.

If we prefix the expression "it is not the case that" to the simple statement "Jones is here," we form the compound statement "it is not the case that Jones is here." This compound statement is called the *negation* or *denial* of the component statement. If we let *A* abbreviate the statement that Jones is here, then the negation of *A* is symbolized as "not-*A*." There are a number of ways in English to form the negation of the statement that Jones is here. We can assert "it is not the case that Jones is here," "it is false that Jones is here," or "Jones is not here." All these statements are symbolized as "not-*A*."

The capital letters *A, B, C,* and so on are used to abbreviate *simple* statements. Thus the expression "not-*A*" is the negation of some *particular simple* statement *A*. The lower case letters *p, q, r,* and so on are not abbreviations of particular statements. They are simply letters in place of which *either a simple or compound statement* may be written.[2] Thus if we wish to say that the negation of *any* statement is symbolized by writing the word "not" in front of the statement, we can express this by saying that the negation of *p* is symbolized as "not-*p*." In place of *p* we can write *any simple or compound statement.*

There are a number of valid argument forms involving negation. Consider the statement "Jones is here." One way to form the negation of this statement is "Jones is not here." To form the negation of this latter statement we can write "it is false that Jones is not here." If we let *A* abbreviate the statement "Jones is here," then "Jones is not here" is symbolized as "not-*A*" and "it is false that Jones is not here" is symbolized as "not-(not-*A*)." Statement *A* and "not-(not-*A*)" are equivalent to one another.

---

2. The letters *A, B, C,* and so on are sometimes called *statement constants* since they are abbreviations of *particular simple* statements. The letters *p, q, r,* and so on are sometimes called *statement variables* since any simple or compound statement can be written in place of them.

Since they are, we may validly infer "not-(not-A)" from A, and from "not-(not-A)" we may validly infer A. The following two very elementary argument forms, which are both called *double negation,* are thus valid.

       (1) p.   (1) Not-(not-p).

    ∴ (2) Not-(not-p).   ∴ (2) p.

Any time we are given the statement p or the statement "not-(not-p)," we may validly infer the double negation of these statements. Some examples of arguments having these forms are:

       (1) Jones is here.

    ∴ (2) It is false that Jones is not here.

       (1) It is not true that we do not do things for other people.

    ∴ (2) We do things for other people.

Another way to form a compound statement is to insert the word "and" between two statements. The resulting compound statement is a *conjunction* and the component statements are *conjuncts.* Hence the compound statement "Jones is here and Smith is on the telephone" is a conjunction. If we let A abbreviate the statement that Jones is here and B abbreviate the statement that Smith is on the telephone, then the compound statement is symbolized as "A and B." More generally, for any two statements p and q, the conjunction of these two statements is symbolized as "p and q."

There are other ways to express a conjunction in English besides using the word "and." The following are all conjunctions:

Jones is here but Smith is on the telephone.
Jones is here although Smith is on the telephone.
Jones is here however Smith is on the telephone.

Sometimes the word "and" does not express a conjunction. For example the statement "John and Bob are roommates" is not a conjunction. It does not state that John is a roommate and Bob is a roommate. Instead the word "and" expresses a relation between John and Bob. However the statement "John and Bob are tall" is a conjunction. It states that John is tall and Bob is tall.

There are a number of valid argument forms involving conjunction. Three very elementary ones are:

$$
\begin{array}{lll}
(1) \quad p. & (1) \quad p \text{ and } q. & (1) \quad p \text{ and } q. \\
(2) \quad q. & \rule{3cm}{0.4pt} & \rule{3cm}{0.4pt} \\
\rule{3.5cm}{0.4pt} & \therefore (2) \quad p. & \therefore (2) \quad q. \\
\therefore (3) \quad p \text{ and } q. &&
\end{array}
$$

The argument form on the left is appropriately called *conjunction.* Any time we are given the statement that p and we are given the statement that q, we may validly infer the conjunctive statement "p and q." Thus if we know that it is cold outside and we know that it is snowing outside, we may deduce that it is both cold and snowing outside. The second two argument forms are both called *simplification.* From a conjunctive statement we may validly infer that either one of the conjuncts is true.

The disjunction of two statements is formed by inserting the word "or" between the two statements. The component statements are called *disjuncts.* Thus the statement "Jones is here or Smith is here" is a disjunction. One problem with disjunctive statements is that the word "or" is ambiguous. Consider the statement that students who receive either an A on their test or on their paper will receive an A in the course. The intended sense of this statement is that any student who gets an A on his test or who gets an A on his paper or who makes an A on the test and on his paper will get an A in the course. This is the *inclusive* sense of "or." In the inclusive sense of "or," the statement "p or q" means "p or q or perhaps both p and q." However the intended sense of "Students who missed the exam may take it Tuesday or Wednesday" is not that a student may take the test on Tuesday, Wednesday, or both on Tuesday and Wednesday. What is intended is that a student may take the test on Tuesday or Wednesday but not on both days. In the *exclusive* sense of "or," the statement "p or q" means "p or q but not both p and q." In the inclusive sense of "or," a disjunctive statement is true just in case *at least* one of the disjuncts is true; however, both of the disjuncts may be true. In the exclusive sense of "or," a disjunctive statement is true if *at least* one of the disjuncts is true and *at most* one of the disjuncts is true. In what follows we will be concerned with the inclusive sense of "or," and we will symbolize disjunctive statements in this sense as "*p* or *q*."

Again there are several valid argument forms involving disjunctive statements. Any argument having one of the forms

(1)	*p* or *q*.	(1)	*p* or *q*.
(2)	Not-*p*.	(2)	Not-*q*.

∴ (3) *q*.   ∴ (3) *p*.

is valid. These valid argument forms will be called *denying one of the disjuncts.*[3] Given a disjunctive statement and the denial of one of the disjuncts, we may validly infer the other disjunct. Thus the following argument is valid.

(1) Either inflation will continue or unemployment will rise.

(2) Inflation will not continue.

∴ (3) Unemployment will rise.

If the premises of the argument are assumed to be true, the conclusion also would have to be true. In order for the disjunctive statement to be true, one of the disjuncts must be true. Premise (2) is the denial of one of the disjuncts. Hence the other disjunct would have to be true.

Statements that have the logical form

If *p,* then *q*

are *conditional statements.* The statement following the "if" is the *antecedent* and the statement following the "then" is the *consequent.* Thus the statement "If Jones has cancer, then he is gravely ill" is a conditional statement. The antecedent is "Jones has cancer" and the consequent is "He is gravely ill." Conditional statements can be expressed in a number of ways in English. Another way to assert the statement "If Jones has cancer, then he

---

3. Sometimes they are called *disjunctive syllogisms.*

is gravely ill" is to say "Jones has cancer only if he is gravely ill." Other ways to express this conditional are: "Jones is gravely ill if he has cancer" and "Jones is gravely ill provided that he has cancer." If we let A abbreviate the statement "Jones has cancer" and B abbreviate "He is gravely ill," then the following all express the conditional statement "If A, then B":

If A, B.
A only if B.
B if A.
B provided that A.

These are just a few of the ways in which we can express a conditional statement in English. However, it is convenient for the purposes of logic to express conditional statements in a uniform way. Thus whenever any of the statements in our above list occur in an argument, we will symbolize them as "If A, then B." Notice that the order of A and B is very important. The statement "Jones has cancer if he is gravely ill" (A if B) expresses the conditional "If B, then A" and not the conditional "If A, then B." The statement "Jones is gravely ill only if he has cancer" (B only if A) expresses the conditional "If B, then A" and not "If A, then B."

More generally, for any two statements p and q, the following expresses the conditional statement "If p, then q":

If p, q.
p only if q.
q if p.
q provided that p.

Thus if we are given a statement having the form "p only if q," we know that this expresses the conditional statement "If p, then q." Whenever we are given a statement having one of the forms in the above list, we will express it in our uniform way as "If p, then q."

A few more examples should be helpful. Consider the statement "The student understands the book provided that the explanations are clear." If we let

A: The explanations are clear.
B: The student understands the book.

then the statement is "*B* provided that *A*." If we express this statement in our uniform way, it becomes "If *A*, then *B*." Next take the statement "The explanations are clear if the student understands the book." Given the abbreviations, the statement is "*A* if *B*." This expresses the conditional statement "If *B*, then *A*."

There are a number of valid argument forms involving conditional statements. The following valid argument form is called *affirming the antecedent*.

> (1) If *p*, then *q*.
> (2) *p*.
>
> ---
>
> ∴ (3) *q*.

Any time we are given a conditional statement and its antecedent, we may validly infer the consequent. If an argument has this form and has true premises, then the conclusion must be true. The argument below is thus valid.

> Students must live up to their responsibilities if they gain equal representation in formulating policies for the university. But students have gained such representation, so they must live up to their responsibilities.

To show that this is a valid argument, let

> *A:* Students gain equal representation in formulating policies for the university.
> *B:* Students must live up to their responsibilities.

The first statement of the argument is "*B* if *A*." This is just another way to express the conditional "If *A*, then *B*." The argument thus can be symbolized as:

> (1) If *A*, then *B*.
> (2) *A*.
>
> ---
>
> ∴ (3) *B*.

Since this argument has a valid argument form, the argument is valid.

It should be remembered that we may replace the letters p, q, r, and so on by either simple or compound statements. Hence in the argument form

> (1) If p, then q.
> (2) p.
> ───────────────────
> ∴ (3) q.

simple or compound statements may be written in place of the letters p and q. The following argument is thus also an example of affirming the antecedent.

> If seeing violence on television does not tend to cause violent behavior in children, then it should be permissible for them to view such violence. Now seeing violence on television does not tend to cause this behavior. Hence it should be acceptable for them to view such violence.

To see that this is an example of affirming the antecedent, let:

> A: Seeing violence on television does tend to cause violent behavior in children.
> B: It should be permissible for children to view violence on television.

The argument is:

> (1) If not-A, then B.
> (2) Not-A.
> ───────────────────
> ∴ (3) B.

(2) is the antecedent of the conditional statement (1), so we may infer (3) by affirming the antecedent.

Another valid argument form involving a conditional statement is *denying the consequent*. Denying the consequent has the form:

> (1) If p, then q.
> (2) Not-q.
> ───────────────────
> ∴ (3) Not-p.

If we are given a conditional statement and the denial of the consequent, we may validly infer the denial of the antecedent. Some examples of arguments having this form are:

> History is a science only if it contains general laws. But history does not contain any such laws. Thus history is not a science.

> Jones must be willing to suffer the consequences of his action if he conscientiously objects to the draft. However he is not willing to suffer the consequences, so he does not conscientiously object to the draft.

Given the symbolization

> *A:* History is a science.
> *B:* History contains general laws.
> *C:* Jones conscientiously objects to the draft.
> *D:* Jones must be willing to suffer the consequences of his action.

the arguments become:

> (1) If *A*, then *B*.
> (2) Not-*B*.
> _____
> ∴ (3) Not-*A*.

> (1) If *C*, then *D*.
> (2) Not-*D*.
> _____
> ∴ (3) Not-*C*.

Since both of these arguments are instances of denying the consequent, they are valid.

The *hypothetical syllogism* is a third valid argument form involving conditional statements. It has the form:

> (1) If *p*, then *q*.
> (2) If *q*, then *r*.
> _____
> ∴ (3) If *p*, then *r*.

Examples of arguments having this form are:

> It is our duty to do some action only if we are able to do it. Now we are able to do some action only if it maximizes our welfare. Hence if it is our duty to do some action, then it maximizes our welfare.

> Jones's action must be a nonviolent violation of the law if it is an act of civil disobedience. If Jones's action is such a nonviolent act, then to be justified it must produce more good than harm. Thus if Jones's action is an act of civil disobedience, then again to be justified it must produce more good than harm.

To show that the first argument is valid, let

> *A:*   It is our duty to do some action.
> *B:*   We are able to do it.
> *C:*   It maximizes our welfare.

then the argument can be symbolized as:

> (1)   If *A*, then *B*.
> (2)   If *B*, then *C*.
> _____
> ∴ (3)   If *A*, then *C*.

Given the symbolization

> *D:*   Jones's action is an act of civil disobedience.
> *E:*   Jones's action is a nonviolent violation of the law.
> *F:*   To be justified it must produce more good than harm.

the second argument is:

> (1)   If *D*, then *E*.
> (2)   If *E*, then *F*.
> _____
> ∴ (3)   If *D*, then *F*.

Both of these arguments are valid since the argument form is valid.

The *dilemma* is a type of argument that involves both conditional and disjunctive statements. All the following valid argument forms are called dilemmas.

(1) p or q.		(1) p or q.
(2) If p, then r.		(2) If p, then r.
(3) If q, then s.		(3) If q, then r.

$\therefore$ (4) r or s. $\qquad\qquad \therefore$ (4) r.

(1) p or not-p.		(1) p or not-p.
(2) If p, then q.		(2) If p, then q.
(3) If not-p, then q.		(3) If not-p, then r.

$\therefore$ (4) q. $\qquad\qquad \therefore$ (4) q or r.

Some examples of dilemmas are:

The General Studies curriculum will be increased if the faculty remains in power. It will be decreased provided that the students gain equal representation. But either the faculty will remain in power or the students will gain equal representation. Therefore either the General Studies curriculum will be increased or decreased.

Either the majority rules or it does not rule in a democracy. If it rules, it is unfair to the minority. But it is unfair to the majority, if it does not rule. Thus it is either unfair to the minority or the majority.

There is bound to be misery in Southeast Asia, for there either will be a military victory or a political victory. But there will be misery if there is a military victory. And if there is a political victory again there will be misery.

If we let

- A: The faculty will remain in power.
- B: The students will gain equal representation.
- C: The General Studies curriculum will be increased.
- D: The General Studies curriculum will be decreased.

Then the first argument is:

> (1) *A* or *B*.
> (2) If *A*, then *C*.
> (3) If *B*, then *D*.
> _____
> ∴ (4) *C* or *D*.

Given that

> *E:* The majority rules in a democracy.
> *F:* It is unfair to the minority.
> *G:* It is unfair to the majority.

the second argument is symbolized as:

> (1) *E* or not-*E*.
> (2) If *E*, then *F*.
> (3) If not-*E*, then *G*.
> _____
> ∴ (4) *F* or *G*.

And letting

> *H:* There will be a military victory.
> *I:* There will be a political victory.
> *J:* There will be misery.

the third argument is:

> (1) *H* or *I*.
> (2) If *H*, then *J*.
> (3) If *I*, then *J*.
> _____
> ∴ (4) *J*.

These three arguments are all valid since they have the valid argument form of a dilemma.

One way to criticize a dilemma is to attack the disjunctive statement. Frequently various alternatives are overlooked. For instance in the first argument above perhaps the students will gain greater representation but not equal representation. This increase in representation may have the effect that the faculty no longer are in control of the university. In this case both disjuncts would be false so the entire disjunctive statement would be false. The new balance of power might result in neither group being able to increase or decrease the General Studies curriculum. When critically evaluating a dilemma make sure that important alternatives have not been overlooked.

Thus far we have considered the valid elementary argument forms of double negation, conjunction, simplification, denying one of the disjuncts, affirming the antecedent, denying the consequent, hypothetical syllogism, and dilemma. Any argument having one of these forms is valid. Thus to show that an argument is valid, it is sufficient to show that it has one of these forms.

Exercises

For each of the following arguments, show that it is valid by showing that it has one of the above valid elementary argument forms.

1. Women will achieve equality only if they accept new responsibilities. Thus if they achieve equality, they must view themselves in a different way than they traditionally have, since they will accept new responsibilities only if they view themselves in a different way than they traditionally have.

2. It is false that Nixon was not president in 1971, so Nixon must have been president in 1971.

3. We must hold very young children morally responsible for their actions if we punish them. We do punish them; hence we must hold them morally responsible for their actions.

4. We will achieve quality education in the United States only if we make the necessary financial commitment. Since we are not making such a commitment, we will not achieve quality education in the United States.

5. Either the fetus is human life or it is just a mass of cells. If the former, then there are only a few circumstances where abortion is justified. If the latter, then all cases of abortion are

justified. Hence either there are only a few circumstances where abortion is justified or all cases of abortion are justified.

6. If we accept abortion on the grounds that the fetus is dependent on the mother, then we ought to be willing to accept doing away with older people who no longer can care for themselves. But we are not willing to accept this, so we cannot accept abortion on the grounds that the fetus is dependent on the mother.

7. Either we will legislate morals by having abortion laws or we will not. If we do, then we restrict the freedom of the female. If we do not, then we fail to protect the rights of the unborn child. Hence either we restrict the freedom of the female or we fail to protect the rights of the unborn child.

8. Either we limit the number of children a family can have or else the population will expand too much. We are not limiting the number of children a family can have, so the population will expand too rapidly.

9. If we accept laws pertaining to robbery, murder, rape, and so on, then we accept legal constraints being placed on a person's morals. But if we accept this, then it is odd that we argue that abortion laws should be done away with for the reason that they "legislate morality." Thus it is odd that we argue that abortion laws should be done away with for the reason that they "legislate morality," if we accept laws pertaining to robbery, murder, rape, and so on.

Answers to Selected Exercises

1. Let

   A: Women will achieve equality.
   B: Women accept new responsibilities.
   C: Women must view themselves in a different way than they traditionally have.

Then the argument is:

     (1) If A, then B.
     (2) If B, then C.

   ∴ (3) If A, then C.

The argument is valid since it is an instance of hypothetical syllogism.

  3. Let

    A: We punish very young children.
    B: We hold very young children morally responsible for their actions.

The argument is:

     (1) If A, then B.
     (2) A.

   ∴ (3) B.

It is an instance of affirming the antecedent.

  5. Let

    A: The fetus is human life.
    B: The fetus is just a mass of cells.
    C: There are only a few circumstances where abortion is justified.
    D: All cases of abortion are justified.

The argument is:

     (1) Either A or B.
     (2) If A, then C.
     (3) If B, then D.

   ∴ (4) Either C or D.

The argument is an example of a dilemma.

  7. Let

    A: We will legislate morals by having abortion laws.

B: We restrict the freedom of the female.
C: We fail to protect the rights of the unborn child.

The argument is:

 (1) Either A or not-A.
 (2) If A, then B.
 (3) If not-A, then C.
 ──────────────────────────
∴ (4) Either B or C.

This is also an instance of a dilemma.

9. Let

A: We accept laws pertaining to robbery, murder, rape, and so on.
B: We accept legal constraints being placed on a person's morals.
C: It is odd that we argue that abortion laws should be done away with for the reason that they "legislate morality."

The argument is an example of a hypothetical syllogism.

 (1) If A, then B.
 (2) If B, then C.
 ──────────────────────────
∴ (3) If A, then C.

2-4 Deductions

If an argument has one of our valid elementary argument forms, it follows that it is valid. Frequently an argument will involve a number of these argument forms. In such cases in order to show that the argument is valid, we have to show that the conclusion can be validly deduced from the premises by appealing to our valid elementary argument forms. An example of an argument that involves more than one of these valid argument forms is:

If abortion is the taking of human life, then abortion is not morally correct. But abortion is morally correct so it cannot be the taking of a human life.

To show that the argument is valid, let

A: Abortion is the taking of a human life.
B: Abortion is morally correct.

Symbolized the argument is:

> (1) If A, then not-B.
> (2) B.
> ─────────────────────────────
> ∴ (3) Not-A.

Notice that strictly speaking this argument is not an instance of denying the consequent. Premise (2) is not the *denial* of the consequent of (1). Remember that the denial or negation of a statement p is "not-p." Hence the denial of "not-B" is "not-(not-B)." To show that this argument is valid then we must deduce the conclusion from the premises by appealing to our valid argument forms. The deduction is as follows: premise (2) yields "not-(not-B)" by double negation. We now have the denial of the consequent of (1). Hence we may deduce the conclusion (3) by denying the consequent. Since the conclusion was validly deduced from the premises, the argument is valid.

Let us take another example:

We will be able to spend more on domestic problems and solve problems at home if we reduce foreign aid. And if we spend more on domestic problems, it will help to solve our racial problems. Since we are reducing foreign aid and stressing our domestic problems, it will help to solve our racial problems.

If the statements in the argument are symbolized as

A: We reduce foreign aid.
B: We will be able to spend more on domestic problems.
C: We will be able to solve problems at home.

D: It will help to solve our racial problems.
E: We are stressing our domestic problems.

then the argument is:

(1)   If *A*, then *B* and *C*.
(2)   If *B*, then *D*.
(3)   *A* and *E*.

∴ (4)   *D*.

This argument brings out an important point. As premise (1) is symbolized it is ambiguous. It could be interpreted as the conditional statement

If *A*, then (*B* and *C*)

where the antecedent is *A* and the consequent is the conjunction "*B* and *C*." Or it could be interpreted as the conjunctive statement

(If *A*, then *B*) and *C*

where the conjuncts are "If *A*, then *B*" and *C*. Parentheses are used to remove the ambiguity. It is clear from the argument that premise (1) should be symbolized in the first way and not the second way. The following statement is also ambiguous:

Jones was there or Smith was there and Doe was absent.

Let

A: Jones was there.
B: Smith was there.
C: Doe was absent.

Without parentheses the compound statement is:

A or *B* and *C*.

This is ambiguous. It can be interpreted either as the disjunctive statement

A or (*B* and *C*)

or as the conjunctive statement

(*A* or *B*) and *C*.

To remove the ambiguity we again employ our parentheses. From now on we will use parentheses to remove any ambiguity that might result in symbolizing compound statements.

Our above argument should thus be symbolized as:

(1)   If *A*, then (*B* and *C*).
(2)   If *B*, then *D*.
(3)   *A* and *E*.

∴ (4)   *D*.

Now how can we deduce the conclusion from the premises? Notice first that from premise (3) we can deduce *A* by simplification. This is the antecedent of the conditional statement "If *A*, then (*B* and *C*)." But any time we are given a conditional statement, whether the antecedent or consequent is a simple or compound statement, and we are given the antecedent, we may validly infer the consequent by the valid argument form of affirming the antecedent.[4] Hence statement *A*, which we deduced from (3), and premise (1) yield "*B* and *C*" by affirming the antecedent. "*B* and *C*" yields statement *B* again by simplification. The conclusion follows from *B* and premise (2) by affirming the antecedent.

A few more examples of deducing the conclusion of an argument from its premises by appealing to our valid elementary argument forms will be helpful. Consider the following argument.

If God is all-knowing then He knows all truths. And He knows all truths only if He knows all future truths. Now if God knows all future truths, it follows He knows what we will do tomorrow. But if He knows this, our actions are determined. However it is obvious that our actions are not determined. Thus God is not all-knowing.

---

4. Remember that *simple or compound* statements may replace *p, q, r,* and so on in our valid elementary argument forms.

To show that the argument is valid, let

> A: God is all-knowing.
> B: He knows all truths.
> C: He knows all future truths.
> D: He knows what we will do tomorrow.
> E: Our actions are determined.

Symbolized the argument is:

> (1)   If A, then B.
> (2)   If B, then C.
> (3)   If C, then D.
> (4)   If D, then E.
> (5)   Not-E.
> _____
>
> ∴ (6)   Not-A.

From premises (1) and (2) we can deduce "If A, then C" by hypothetical syllogism. This statement and (3) yield "If A, then D," and this latter statement and (4) yield "If A, then E" both by hypothetical syllogism. From "If A, then E" and (5) we can deduce the conclusion by denying the consequent. The conclusion thus has been validly deduced from the premises. Notice that repeated application of denying the consequent also would yield the conclusion.

The next argument involves several valid argument forms too.

> Either our actions are causally determined or they are not. If they are, then our actions are not free. But if our actions are not free, then we are not morally responsible for them. On the other hand if our actions are not causally determined, then we do not have causal control over our actions. But if we do not, then again we are not morally responsible for them. If we do not have such responsibility, we cannot be blamed for our actions. Hence we cannot be blamed for our actions.

Using the abbreviations

> A: Our actions are causally determined.

    B: Our actions are free.
    C: We are morally responsible for our actions.
    D: We have causal control over our actions.
    E: We can be blamed for our actions.

the argument becomes:

        (1) *A* or not-*A.*
        (2) If *A,* then not-*B.*
        (3) If not-*B,* then not-*C.*
        (4) If not-*A,* then not-*D.*
        (5) If not-*D,* then not-*C.*
        (6) If not-*C,* then not-*E.*

∴ (7) Not-*E.*

From premises (2) and (3) we can deduce "If *A,* then not-*C*" by hypothetical syllogism. We also can deduce "If not-*A,* then not-*C*" from (4) and (5) by hypothetical syllogism. Given premise (1) this yields "not-*C*" by dilemma. "Not-*C*" and (6) yield (7) by affirming the antecedent. Hence the argument is valid.

Exercises

Show that the arguments below are valid.

1. Women's liberation is true liberation only if the women involved in the movement do not try to impose their will on all women. But that is exactly what they are doing, so it is certainly not true liberation.

2. An open admissions policy must be established in the universities. In a democratic society such as ours a college education is very important. But if so, then everyone ought to have the right to come to college. An open admissions policy must be established in the universities if this is true.

3. If God, an all-good, powerful, and knowing being exists, this must be the best of all possible worlds. It is the best of all possible worlds only if there is no unnecessary evil. But there is unnecessary evil everywhere. Thus God does not exist.

4. Computers can be said to think only if they are rational beings. But if they are rational beings, they deserve civil rights. However it is clear that they do not merit such rights, so we cannot say that they think.

5. In general it is wrong to destroy human life. However the fetus is clearly human life. If these two statements are true, then abortion is wrong. But if abortion is wrong, then we have legalized something immoral and we have made a great mistake. It follows that we have made a great mistake.

6. Either mathematical truths are empirically true or they are true by definition. If they are empirically true, then to verify them we have to appeal to empirical evidence. But to verify them we do not have to appeal to empirical evidence at all. Thus they must be true by definition.

7. Either you get drafted or you resist the draft and go to prison. If the former, your freedom is severely restricted. If the latter, your freedom is again severely restricted. Thus your freedom is going to be restricted.

8. There is an important question as to whether the fetus is human life. If there were no such question, then an abortion would be like having your appendix removed. And it would be like this only if there were no moral controversy. But there is such a controversy.

9. If statements about God are empirically meaningful, they must in principle be empirically verifiable. Such statements are empirically verifiable only if there is in principle evidence that would tend to support or disconfirm them. There is no such evidence. Hence such statements are not empirically meaningful. If they are not, they are just expressions of emotions. It follows that such statements are just expressions of emotions.

Answers to Selected Exercises

1. Let

    A: Women's liberation is true liberation.
    B: The women involved in the movement do try to impose their will on all women.

Then the argument is:

> (1) If *A*, then not-*B*.
> (2) *B*.
> _____
> ∴ (3) Not-*A*.

Note that (2) is not the denial of the consequent of (1). But (2) yields the denial "not-(not-*B*)" by double negation. (3) follows from this statement and (1) by denying the consequent.

3. Let

> *A:* God, an all-good, powerful, and knowing being exists.
> *B:* This must be the best of all possible worlds.
> *C:* There is unnecessary evil.

The argument is:

> (1) If *A*, then *B*.
> (2) If *B*, then not-*C*.
> (3) *C*.
> _____
> ∴ (4) Not-*A*.

(1) and (2) yield "If *A*, then not-*C*" by hypothetical syllogism. (3) yields "not-(not-*C*)" by double negation. This statement and "If *A*, then not-*C*" yield (4) by denying the consequent. Double negation and two steps of denying the consequent also would yield (4).

5. Let

> *A:* In general it is wrong to destroy human life.
> *B:* The fetus is human life.
> *C:* Abortion is wrong.
> *D:* We have legalized something immoral.
> *E:* We have made a great mistake.

The argument is:

> (1) *A.*

(2) *B.*
(3) If *A* and *B*, then *C.*
(4) If *C*, then (*D* and *E*).

∴ (5) *E.*

Premises (1) and (2) yield "*A* and *B*" by conjunction. This statement and (3) yield *C*, and *C* and (4) yield "*D* and *E*" both by affirming the antecedent. The conclusion (5) follows from this latter statement by simplification.

7. Let

    A: You get drafted.
    B: You resist the draft.
    C: You go to prison.
    D: Your freedom is severely restricted.

Then the argument is:

(1) *A* or (*B* and *C*).
(2) If *A*, then *D.*
(3   If *B* and *C*, then *D.*

∴ (4) *D.*

This is an example of a dilemma so the argument is valid.

9. Let

    A: Statements about God are empirically meaningful.
    B: Statements about God are in principle empirically verifiable.
    C: There is in principle evidence that would tend to support or disconfirm them.
    D: Statements about God are just expressions of emotion.

The argument is:

(1) If *A*, then *B.*
(2) If *B*, then *C.*

    (3) Not-*C*.
∴ (4) Not-*A*.
    (5) If not-*A*, then *D*.

∴ (6) *D*.

Premises (1) and (2) yield "If *A*, then *C*" by hypothetical syllo-gism. (4) follows from "If *A*, then *C*" and premise (3) by denying the consequent. (6) follows from (4) and (5) by affirming the antecedent.

2-5 Invalidity

In this section we discuss a technique for showing that an argu-ment is invalid. Suppose that someone argued:

    (1) Either students will gain equal representa-tion in the governance of the university or the outdated curriculum will continue.
    (2) The students will gain equal representation in the governance of the university.

∴ (3) The outdated curriculum will not continue.

To show that the argument is invalid we might respond by saying that this argument has the same form as the following argument.

    (1) Either Lincoln was president or Nixon was president.
    (2) Lincoln was president.

∴ (3) Nixon was not president.

This latter argument is clearly invalid since it has true premises and a false conclusion. Since this latter argument is invalid and the two arguments have the same form, the first argument is invalid too.

    To show that the original argument was invalid, we constructed a second argument having the same logical form as the first where the second argument had true premises and a false conclusion. This method of proving invalidity is called *refutation by logical analogy.*[5] The reason this is an effective means of proving invalidity is that invalidity, like validity, is a formal property of arguments. An argument is invalid by virtue of its logical form alone. If two arguments have the same logical form and one of them is invalid, it follows that the other argument is also invalid even though the subject matter of the argument is different.

Let us explain the method of refutation by logical analogy in more detail. To show that an argument is invalid, proceed in the following way. First, let the capital letters A, B, C, and so on be abbreviations of the simple statements in the argument. Second, symbolize the argument using the abbreviations. Third, replace the capital letters A, B, C, and so on by the letters p, q, r, and so on. Wherever A occurs in the argument, p is to replace it. Wherever B occurs in the argument, q is to replace it. The same procedure is to be followed for C, D, and any other capital letter that occurs in the symbolized argument. What is revealed by this process of substitution is the form of the argument. Finally, produce another argument having the same exact form where the premises of this argument are true and yet the conclusion is false. Since an argument is invalid by virtue of its logical form alone, this shows that the original argument is invalid.[6] Consider the student example above. Let

> A: The students will gain equal representation in the governance of the university.
> B: The outdated curriculum will continue.

Then the argument is:

> (1) A or B.
> (2) A.
> _____
> $\therefore$ (3) Not-B.

If we replace A by p and B by q, then the form of the argument is:

---

5. Sometimes it is called refutation by counterexample.
6. To make this procedure completely effective some refinements are needed. The interested reader should consult Irving M. Copi, *Introduction to Logic*, 4th ed. (New York: Macmillan, 1972), pp. 267-70.

(1) p or q.
(2) p.

$\therefore$ (3) Not-q.

The argument

(1) Either Lincoln was president or Nixon was president.
(2) Lincoln was president.

$\therefore$ (3) Nixon was not president.

has the same logical form and has true premises and a false conclusion. Since it is invalid and has the same logical form, it follows that the original argument is invalid.

There are a few invalid argument forms that are often confused with the valid argument forms of affirming the antecedent and denying the consequent. Consider the argument:

(1) If students are on the Curriculum Committee, General Studies will be reduced.
(2) General Studies was reduced.

$\therefore$ (3) Students must be on the Curriculum Committee.

If we let

A: Students are on the Curriculum Committee.
B: General Studies is reduced.

then the argument is:

(1) If A, then B.
(2) B.

$\therefore$ (3) A.

When we replace A and B by p and q, the form of the argument is:

(1) If p, then q.
(2) q.

∴ (3) p.

An argument that has the same logical form and has true premises and a false conclusion is:

(1) If Richard Nixon is a bachelor, then he is a man.
(2) He is a man.

∴ (3) Richard Nixon is a bachelor.

Thus the original argument is invalid. This fallacious argument form is called the fallacy of *affirming the consequent.* Be careful not to confuse the invalid argument form of affirming the consequent with the valid argument form of affirming the antecedent.

Another argument form that is fallacious is *denying the antecedent.* One might argue:

(1) If students are on the Curriculum Committee, General Studies will be reduced.
(2) Students are not on the Curriculum Committee.

∴ (3) General Studies will not be reduced.

Given the abbreviations

A: Students are on the Curriculum Committee.
B: General Studies will be reduced.

the argument is:

(1) If A, then B.
(2) Not-A.

∴ (3) Not-B.

Replacing A and B by p and q, the argument has the form:

(1) If *p*, then *q*.
(2) Not-*p*.

∴ (3) Not-*q*.

The following argument has the same form and is clearly invalid since it has true premises and a false conclusion:

(1) If Richard Nixon is a bachelor, then he is a man.
(2) Richard Nixon is not a bachelor.

∴ (3) He is not a man.

Again one should be careful not to confuse the invalid argument form of denying the antecedent with the valid argument form of denying the consequent.

A few more examples should be helpful. Suppose it were argued:

Either young men are drafted or else they serve their country in another way. But they serve against their will if they are drafted. And if they serve against their will, then it is not in the interest of the nation. Thus it is in the interest of the nation if they serve their country in another way.

Let

A: Young men are drafted.
B: They serve their country in another way.
C: They serve against their will.
D: It is in the interest of the nation.

The argument is:

(1) *A* or *B*.
(2) If *A*, then *C*.
(3) If *C*, then not-*D*.

∴ (4) If *B*, then *D*.

Replacing *A, B, C,* and *D* by *p, q, r,* and *s* respectively, the form of the argument is:

> (1) *p* or *q*.
> (2) If *p*, then *r*.
> (3) If *r*, then not-*s*.
>
> ---
>
> ∴ (4) If *q*, then *s*.

An argument that has this form and also has true premises and a false conclusion is:

> (1) Richard Nixon was either mayor of New York City or president of the United States.
> (2) If he was mayor of New York City, then he had a difficult job.
> (3) If he had a difficult job, then the job was not easy.
>
> ---
>
> ∴ (4) If he was president of the United States, then the job was easy.

For the final example consider the argument:

> Jones's act is an act of civil disobedience only if Jones is willing to accept the consequences of his act. If he is willing to accept these consequences, then either he must be willing to go to jail or at least to stand trial for his violation of the law. But he is not willing to go to jail, so his act was not an act of civil disobedience.

If we abbreviate the simple statements as:

> *A:* Jones's act is an act of civil disobedience.
> *B:* Jones is willing to accept the consequences of his act.
> *C:* He is willing to go to jail.
> *D:* He is willing at least to stand trial for his violation of the law.

then the argument is:

(1) If *A*, then *B*.
(2) If *B*, then (*C* or *D*).
(3) Not-*C*.

∴ (4) Not-*A*.

Replacing the letters *A*, *B*, *C*, and *D*, the result is:

(1) If *p*, then *q*.
(2) If *q*, then (*r* or *s*).
(3) Not-*r*.

∴ (4) Not-*p*.

An obviously invalid argument with this form is:

(1) If Richard Nixon is married, then he is human.
(2) If he is human, then he is dead or he is living.
(3) He is not dead.

∴ (4) He is not married.

The techniques developed in this chapter are limited to arguments where the validity or invalidity of the argument depends on the way simple statements are combined to form compound statements. These techniques do not apply to all arguments. Take the following example:

(1) All men are mortal.
(2) Socrates is a man.

∴ (3) Socrates is mortal.

If we let

A: All men are mortal.
B: Socrates is a man.
C: Socrates is mortal.

then the argument is:

   (1) *A.*
   (2) *B.*
   _____
   ∴ (3) *C.*

Given the techniques developed so far for showing validity and
invalidity, we would have to conclude that this argument is invalid. Nevertheless this argument is valid. The validity of the
argument does not depend on the way simple statements are
combined into compound statements, for there are no compound
statements in this argument. Instead the validity of the argument
depends on the inner logical structure of the simple statements. In
this book we shall not consider techniques for demonstrating the
validity or invalidity of such arguments. The interested reader
should consult one of the deductive logic books mentioned in the
bibliography.

Exercises

A. Show that the following arguments are invalid.

   1. If all men are equal, they ought to be treated alike. Thus if all
men ought to be treated alike, they must all be equal.

   2. We have rights only if we are entitled to make various
demands. Thus we have rights and are entitled to make various
demands.

   3. It is not the case that the United States can both police the
world and solve its domestic problems at home. Thus we cannot
police the world and we cannot solve our domestic problems.

   4. You cannot be completely free and also a responsible person.
Since you are not completely free, you are a responsible person.

B. Do the same for the following more complex arguments.

   1. If we are to achieve equal opportunity for all, then either the
federal government has to increase spending on domestic problems
or large private corporations must help. But such corporations are

not going to help, so we are not going to achieve equal opportunity for all.

2. If people are morally responsible for their actions, they must have freedom of will. But if determinism is true, then all actions are caused. And again if determinism is true, we do not have freedom of will. Thus if we are morally responsible for our actions, not all actions are caused.

3. Either we do away with the present grading system or students will continue to be alienated. But if we do away with the present grading system, our academic standards will drop. On the other hand, if students continue to be alienated, they will not get as much out of their education as they otherwise might. Now our academic standards will not drop, so it is not the case that either we must do away with the present grading system or the students will continue to be alienated.

4. If a person violates the law and he is mentally ill, then the person is not legally responsible for his actions. But he cannot be punished if he is not legally responsible for his actions. Thus a person must be mentally ill if he is not legally responsible for his actions.

Answers to Selected Exercises

A.

1. Let

   A: All men are equal.
   B: They ought to be treated alike.

The argument is:

(1)   If *A*, then *B*.
_____

∴ (2)   If *B*, then *A*.

An argument with the same form and with a true premise and a false conclusion is:

> (1) If Richard Nixon is a bachelor, then he is a male.
>
> ∴ (2) If Richard Nixon is a male, then he is a bachelor.

3. Let

    A: The United States can police the world.
    B: The United States can solve its domestic problems at home.

The argument is:

> (1) Not-(*A* and *B*).
>
> ∴ (2) Not-*A* and not-*B*.

An obviously invalid argument with the same form is:

> (1) It is not the case that both Nixon and Kennedy were president in 1973.
>
> ∴ (2) Nixon was not president in 1973 and Kennedy was not president in 1973.

B.

1. Let

    A: We are going to achieve equal opportunity for all.
    B: The federal government has to increase spending on domestic problems.
    C: Large private corporations must help.

Then the argument is:

> (1) If *A*, then (*B* or *C*).
> (2) Not-*C*.
>
> ∴ (3) Not-*A*.

Replacing A, B, and C by p, q, and r, the form of the argument is:

> (1) If p, then (q or r).
> (2) Not-r.
> _____
> ∴ (3) Not-p.

An argument with this form that has true premises and a false conclusion is:

> (1) If Richard Nixon is married, then he has been married only once or more than once.
> (2) He has not been married more than once.
> _____
> ∴ (3) Richard Nixon is not married.

3. Let

- A: We do away with the present grading system.
- B: Students will continue to be alienated.
- C: Our academic standards will drop.
- D: Students will get as much out of their education as they otherwise might.

The argument is:

> (1) A or B.
> (2) If A, then C.
> (3) If B, then not-D.
> (4) Not-C.
> _____
> ∴ (5) Not-(A or B).

And the form of the argument is:

> (1) p or q.
> (2) If p, then r.
> (3) If q, then not-s.
> (4) not-r.
> _____
> ∴ (5) Not-(p or q).

An argument having this form with true premises and a false conclusion is:

    (1)   Either Mao or Nixon is president of the United States in 1973.

    (2)   If Mao is president, then he is a citizen of this country.

    (3)   If Nixon is president, then he was not defeated in the election.

    (4)   Mao is not a citizen of this country.

∴ (5)   It is not the case that either Mao or Nixon is president of the United States in 1973.

2-6 Summary of Basic Concepts

1. An argument is *valid* just in case it is not possible for the premises to be true and the conclusion false. Thus an argument is valid just in case the conclusion must be true if the premises are true.

2. The *logical form* of a statement or argument has to do with its structure, not its subject matter. An argument is valid or invalid by virtue of its logical form alone.

3. To show that an argument is valid, show that it has a valid elementary argument form or that the conclusion can be validly deduced from the premises by appealing only to valid argument forms.

4. To show that an argument is invalid, use the method of *refutation by logical analogy.* Let the capital letters A, B, C, and so on abbreviate the simple statements in the argument. Symbolize the argument in terms of the abbreviations. Next, replace the letters A, B, C, and so on by the letters p, q, r, and so on. This reveals the logical form of the argument. Finally, produce an argument with the same form that has true premises and a false conclusion.

Exercises

Carefully explain your answers and give examples whenever appropriate.

1. Can a valid argument have a false conclusion?

2. Can a valid argument have a false premise?

3. If an argument is invalid, does it follow that it has a false conclusion?

4. Carefully explain the difference between validity and truth.

5. What is the main reason for being interested in validity?

6. If we are concerned with whether an argument conclusively proves a conclusion, what two questions should be asked?

7. What is a compound statement?

8. If two arguments have the same logical form and one of them is valid, does it follow that the other argument is valid?

9. The letters A, B, C, and so on and the letters p, q, r, and so on were used in different ways. What is the difference?

10. Is "Jones is here" the negation of "Jones is not here"?

11. Would "if p, then q," "q provided that p," and "p if q" all express the same statement?

12. In the exclusive sense of "or" is the following a valid argument form?

> (1) p or q.
> (2) p.
> _____
> ∴ (3) Not-q.

13. Is it valid in the inclusive sense?

14. Are the following argument forms valid in the inclusive sense of "or"?

> (1) p.   (1) p or q.
> _____   _____
> ∴ (2) p or q.   ∴ (2) p.

15. Does "not-(not-p and not-q)" express what "p and q" expresses?

16. Does "not-(not-p and not-q)" express what "p or q" expresses?

17. Is the following a valid argument form?

(1) If p, then q.

∴ (2) If not-q, then not-p.

18. Which argument forms are invalid?

affirming the antecedent
denying the antecedent
affirming the consequent
denying the consequent

Inductive Logic

3-1 Inductive Strength

Inductive reasoning is very important since a great number of our beliefs about the world cannot be justified on the basis of deductive arguments alone. Jones might assert that it is probable that it will rain today and to justify his belief argue:

> (1) Most often whenever there is a low pressure area, the temperature is warm, and there is sufficient moisture in the air, it rains.
> (2) These conditions presently exist.
> _____
> ∴ (3) It will probably rain.

This argument is not deductively valid. To justify his belief Jones had to give an inductive argument. Notice also that if Jones were called upon to justify premise (1), he again would have to give an inductive argument. He might argue:

> (1) Most often in the past whenever there was a low pressure area, the temperature was warm, and there was sufficient moisture in the air, it rained.
> _____
> ∴ (2) It is probable that most often whenever

there is a low pressure area, the temperature
is warm, and there is sufficient moisture in
the air, it rains.

The most important notion in inductive logic is that of inductive
strength. An argument is said to be *inductively strong* just in case
(1) it is not deductively valid, and (2) if the premises are true, then
the conclusion is probable.[1] A deductively valid argument with
true premises conclusively proves the conclusion while an inductively strong argument with true premises does not. Instead the
conclusion is made probable. Notice that clause (1) of the definition entails that deductively valid arguments are not to be classified as inductively strong. According to our definition an argument cannot be both deductively valid and inductively strong.

There is another important difference between deductively valid
and inductively strong arguments besides the degree of support
given to the conclusion. If an argument is valid, then adding
further premises does not alter the validity of the argument. As
long as the original argument is valid, we may add as many
premises as we like without destroying the argument's validity.
This is not true in the case of inductively strong arguments.
Further evidence may make the conclusion more probable or it
may make it less probable. When dealing with inductive arguments, additional evidence is very important.[2]

There is a popular misconception that inductive reasoning proceeds from the specific to the general while deductive reasoning
proceeds from the general to the specific.[3] This is true in *some*
cases. For example if we examine a number of people who have
taken LSD and we find chromosome damage, we might inductively infer that taking LSD results in chromosome damage. Here we
proceed from the specific to the general. If we know that all
soldiers returning from combat duty in Vietnam have difficulty in
adjusting to civilian life, we might deductively infer that since
Jones is returning from such combat duty, he too will have
difficulty in adjusting. Here we proceed from the general to the
specific. But the above characterization of inductive and deductive

1. Some authors call such arguments "inductively valid." We shall reserve the term
"valid" for deductively valid arguments.
2. For further discussion of this point see pp. 76-79.
3. See the dictionary entry under "induction" in *Webster's New Collegiate Dictionary*, 2d ed. (Springfield, Mass.: G. and C. Merriam, 1960), p. 427.

reasoning is not true for *all* cases. The exercises at the end of section 4 of chapter 2 clearly demonstrate that not every deductive argument proceeds from the general to the specific, and the first two arguments of the present chapter show that not every inductive argument proceeds from the specific to the general.

In chapter 2 we distinguished deductive validity and truth. Inductive strength and truth also must be distinguished. The inductive strength of an argument has to do with the logical relation between the premises and conclusion. The inductive logician asks: If the premises of an argument are assumed to be true, would the conclusion be probable? The inductive strength of an argument depends on how probable the conclusion is given the truth of the premises. Consider the arguments:

> (1) No man has run the mile in less than two minutes.
> (2) Jones is a man.
> _____
> ∴ (3) Jones will not run the mile in less than two minutes.

> (1) Most men have not run the mile in less than two minutes.
> (2) Jones is a man.
> _____
> ∴ (3) Jones will not run the mile in less than two minutes.

> (1) A few men have not run the mile in less than two minutes.
> (2) Jones is a man.
> _____
> ∴ (3) Jones will not run the mile in less than two minutes.

The first argument is inductively stronger than the other two arguments. If we assume that the premises of the first argument are true, the conclusion is not guaranteed to be true but it is made very probable. Assuming the premises of the second argument are true makes the conclusion probable although not as probable as in the first argument. The truth of the premises of the third argument does not make the conclusion at all probable. Inductively it is the weakest of the three arguments.

When we are interested in whether an argument makes a conclusion probable, there are two questions we should ask. First, is the argument inductively strong? Second, are the premises true? If the argument is not inductively strong, the conclusion has not been shown to be probable. If at least one of the premises is false, again the conclusion has not been shown to be probable.

It might be thought that the conclusion of an inductive argument should contain a qualifying expression such as "it is probable that," "it is almost certain that," "it is quite likely that," "there is very little chance that," "it is almost impossible that." Such qualifying expressions, however, should not be viewed as part of the conclusion. The conclusion of the first argument above is not "It is probable that Jones will not run the mile in less than two minutes." The conclusion is simply "Jones will not run the mile in less than two minutes." The qualifying expression "it is probable that" refers to the logical relation between the premises and the conclusion and indicates the degree of support the premises supposedly give the conclusion.

Quite often the conclusion of a deductive argument will contain the qualifying expression "must." For example it might be argued:

    (1)   All Frenchmen are European.
    (2)   Jones is a Frenchman.
    _____
∴ (3)   Jones must be European.

Again the qualifying expression "must" should not be viewed as being part of the conclusion. The conclusion is "Jones is European." The "must" refers to the logical relation that holds between the premises and conclusion. It indicates that the logical relation is such that if the premises were true, then the conclusion would have to be true. To make the relational aspect of the qualifying expression "must" explicit, we can express the argument as:

"Jones is European" must be true if the premises "All Frenchmen are European" and "Jones is a Frenchman" are true.

The same can be done in order to make the relational character of "it is probable that" explicit. We can write:

"Jones will not run the mile in less than two minutes" is probable if the premises "No man has run the mile in less than two minutes" and "Jones is a man" are true.

In order to make explicit the relational character of qualifying expressions for inductive arguments, we shall place the qualifying expression within parentheses and write it to the right of the last premise.[4] Thus we shall write:

(1) No man has run the mile in less than two minutes.
(2) Jones is a man.   (make highly probable)

∴ (3) Jones will not run the mile in less than two minutes.

Inductive strength, unlike deductive validity, is not a formal property. It is not a property an argument has by virtue of its logical form alone. Certain nonformal conditions also must be satisfied if an argument is to be inductively strong. We shall examine several common inductive argument forms and the nonformal conditions that must be satisfied in order for an argument having one of these forms to be inductively strong.

3-2 Inductive Generalization

One common type of inductive argument is *inductive generalization.* It has the form:

(1) X percent of the observed members of the class S have the property P. (   )

∴ (2) X percent of the members of the class S have the property P.

---

4. This way of making the relational character of qualifying expressions explicit is taken from Carl G. Hempel, *Aspects of Scientific Explanation* (New York: The Free Press, 1965), p. 383.

Here a conclusion about the class S is derived from a premise referring to *observed* members of that class. If X is 100 or 0, the inductive generalization is a *universal* generalization; if X is greater than 0 but less than 100, it is a *statistical* generalization.

Suppose we are considering the effectiveness of a new form of birth control. We could take a number of people and have them use the device. Imagine the result of this test is that when the device was used properly 98 percent of the people found it to be effective. On the basis of this test we might infer that when the device is used properly, 98 percent of the people using it will find it to be effective. Put in standard form this statistical generalization becomes:

> (1) 98 percent of the people in the test who properly used the device found it to be an effective means of birth control.(makes probable)
> _____
> ∴ (2) 98 percent of the people who properly use the device will find it to be an effective means of birth control.

An example of a universal generalization is:

> (1) 100 percent of the cars tested using the new antipollution emission control produced 60 percent less air pollution than the average car not using the emission control.(makes probable)
> _____
> ∴ (2) 100 percent of all the cars using the new antipollution emission control produce 60 percent less air pollution than the average car not using the emission control.

In both examples it is inferred from the premise that a certain percentage of the observed members of a class S have a property P, that approximately the same percentage of all the members of S have P.

Frequently when we encounter inductive generalizations they are not expressed in numerical terms. It might be argued that it is probable that no man can run the mile in less than two minutes since no man has ever done it. This is a universal generalization, and so is:

(1) All recorded past wars have involved the killing of a great number of innocent people such as children. (makes probable)

∴ (2) All wars involve the killing of a great number of innocent people such as children.

Statistical generalizations are expressed in a number of ways. It might be argued that almost all (most, a large number, the majority, quite a few, some, practically none) of the observed members of S have the property $P;$ thus it is probable that almost all (most, a large number, the majority, quite a few, some, practically none) of the members of S have P.

In order for an inductive generalization to be inductively strong, certain nonformal conditions must be satisfied. Two of these conditions have to do with the sample upon which the generalization is based. The observed members of class S form a subset of this class. Call this subset a *sample*. The class S from which the sample is drawn will be called the *population*. We are all familiar with sampling. If we drive a car around the block prior to buying it, we are sampling the performance. When we quickly skip through a book reading parts here and there to determine whether we want to read the whole book, we are again sampling. Whenever we attempt to determine whether a class of things such as events, people, or objects have a certain property on the basis of examining part of that class, we are sampling.

Unless we examine the entire population from which a sample has been drawn, we cannot determine decisively whether or not the sample is representative of that population. However, sampling techniques have been developed that can help us to avoid biased or unrepresentative samples. A classic example of a biased sample is the 1936 preelection presidential poll conducted by the *Literary Digest.* A sample was selected from telephone listings and from a list of subscribers to the magazine. The result of the poll was that Alfred Landon would easily defeat Franklin Roosevelt. Actually it was a landslide victory for Roosevelt. The error was due to the fact that the sample was very unrepresentative of the total voting population. In the depression year of 1936 the majority of the people who could afford telephones and magazines voted Republican. Thus the sample did not represent a cross section of the voters.

A fundamental concept in sampling theory is that of a *random sample*. A random sample is a sample that is selected by a process whereby each member of the population has an equal chance of being included in the sample. We might want to determine how the students at a particular university feel about abortion. If we went to one of the dormitories at ten o'clock in the morning and took a poll of the students living there, our sample would not be a random sample. The sampling technique would not provide an equal chance for each student at the university to be included in the sample. It would rule out students who were at class and those students who lived off campus. One technique that would produce a random sample would be to place all the student identification cards in a container making sure they were completely shuffled, and then to randomly draw out cards reshuffling the cards after each drawing. Each student would have an equal chance of being included in the sample so it would be a random sample. More refined techniques that ensure randomization have been developed using random digits.

A variation of the random sample is the *stratified random sample*. To use our student poll example again, assume the student population consists of 2,000 male and 1,000 female students and that the proportion of these male students opposed to abortion is greater than the proportion of the female students opposed to it. In this case if our sample consisted of more women than men, there is a good chance it would not be representative of the total population. To overcome the problem the population is divided into different subclasses or strata. Then students from these different subclasses are randomly selected to form a random sample. Since there is a greater proportion of males than females in the population, this proportion must be reflected in the sample. Hence if we randomly selected 200 female students, we would have to randomly select 400 male students. The stratified random sample ensures that the sample will include the same proportion of members of the different subclasses or strata as the original population. Stratified random samples should be used when there are subclasses of the population where nonproportionality of these subclasses in the sample would greatly affect the sample with respect to the property in which we are interested.

Sampling techniques such as random sampling and stratified random sampling help us to avoid unrepresentative samples. These procedures do not guarantee that our samples are representative. There is always some risk that they are not. However if we use these techniques, it is less likely that our samples will be biased.

The size of the sample is also important when considering whether the sample is representative of the population. In general the larger the sample size, the greater the probability that the sample will be representative of the population. In our above example if we took a stratified random sample of only thirty students—twenty male and ten female students—the sample would not be of sufficient size to be reliable. A sample of six hundred—four hundred male and two hundred female students—would be more reliable.

Exactly when a sample is of sufficient size to be reliable depends basically on the degree of precision required, the subject matter under investigation, and our background knowledge. If we are conducting a poll on student attitudes toward abortion our sample should be very large. We know that attitudes on abortion vary greatly so our sample has to be fairly large if it is to be reliable. The larger it is the more accurate it will be. On the other hand, suppose we want to determine the sound level inside a certain model of a brand of car when it is driven on various types of roads. The population in this case is the set of all the cars of that particular model and brand. We know from past experience that cars of the same model and brand tend to be very much alike with regard to ride and noise level inside the car. Thus our sample size does not have to be very large in order to be reliable.

If the sample size is not sufficiently large to be reliable, the inductive generalization based on the sample will not be inductively strong. The argument will be fallacious since the premise will not adequately support the conclusion. The *fallacy of insufficient sample size* is the fallacy of basing an inductive generalization upon a sample of insufficient size to be reliable.

The *fallacy of a biased sample* is the fallacy of basing an inductive generalization on a sampling procedure that is likely to make the sample unrepresentative of the population from which it is drawn. In order for an inductive generalization to be inductively strong, we must not rely on such sampling procedures. If we do, the argument will be fallacious.

To summarize, two of the nonformal conditions that must be satisfied if an inductive generalization is to be inductively strong are: (1) The sample must be of sufficient size to be reliable. (2) We must not rely on sampling procedures that are likely to make the sample unrepresentative of its population. A third condition will be discussed in the next section.[5]

Exercises

A. Explain why each of the following inductive generalizations is inductively strong or why it is not.

1. A random sample of 200 students selected from the approximately 1,000 students who had taken a pass-fail course revealed that a majority of the students in the sample felt they had learned more in the pass-fail course than in classes that were not pass-fail. Thus it is probable that the majority of the students who had taken a pass-fail course felt the same way.

2. Robert Tryon took a large random sample of rats and ran them through a maze. Some learned it quickly while it took others a longer time. He bred the bright rats with other bright rats and the dull rats with other dull rats. This was done for nine generations. At the end of this time the slowest of the bright rats took less time in getting through mazes than the fastest of the dull rats. Thus it is probable that selective breeding (eugenics) affects intelligence in rats.[6]

3. It was long believed that highly intelligent young people tended to be physically weak, antisocial, and to become mentally defective in later years. In 1921 L. M. Terman started to gather data on more than 1000 children living mainly in California with IQ's primarily between 140 and 170. The study revealed that these

5. For an elementary introduction to statistics see Jimmy R. Amos, Foster Lloyd Brown, and Oscar G. Mink, *Statistical Concepts: A Basic Program* (New York: Harper and Row, 1965). A more comprehensive introduction is W. Allen Wallis and Harry V. Roberts, *Statistics: A New Approach* (New York: The Free Press, 1956). An enjoyable discussion of statistical fallacies is Darrell Huff, *How to Lie with Statistics* (New York: W. W. Norton, 1954).

6. Frank Cox, *Psychology* (Dubuque, Iowa: Wm. C. Brown, 1970), p. 191.

young people were physically superior to the general population, socially adjusted, and continued to be mentally superior. Thus it is probable that the common beliefs about the gifted are false.[7]

4. A random sample of private colleges across the nation revealed that most of the students were opposed to the death penalty. They thought that if it was wrong for an individual to kill, then it was wrong for society to kill. Thus it is probable that most college students feel the same way.

5. Do television networks present the news in an unbiased way? Edith Effron of *TV Guide* decided to find out. She taped the news shows of ABC, CBS, and NBC during the 1968 presidential campaign. She then analyzed the coverage and found that the three networks gave approximately four times more favorable words to Hubert Humphrey than to Richard Nixon. Miss Effron concluded that the networks unanimously "give preferential status to certain political positions and opinions."[8]

6. John B. Watson, the famous behaviorist, conditioned a two-year-old boy named Albert to fear a white rat. He first encouraged the boy to play with the white rat. After this initial period, when the child would reach for the rat, Watson would suddenly hit a steel bar with a hammer. The noise frightened the child. Soon the child came to fear the rat. Watson generalized that he could thus control behavior by arranging a sequence of conditioned responses. He said:

> Give me a dozen healthy infants, well formed, and my own special world to bring them up in, and I'll guarantee to take any one at random and train him to become any type of specialist I might select; doctor, lawyer, artist, merchant-chief and yes, even beggarman and thief, regardless of his talents, penchant, tendencies, abilities, vocations, and race of his ancestry.[9]

B. You are concerned with how the majority of people in the United States feel about the war in Indochina. A random survey is

---

7. Ronald C. Johnson and Gene R. Medinnus, *Child Psychology* (New York: John Wiley, 1969), pp. 201-3.
8. "Tracking the One-Eyed Monster," *Reader's Digest,* February 1972, pp. 7-8.
9. Quoted in Robert F. Biehler, *Psychology Applied to Teaching* (Boston: Houghton Mifflin, 1971), p. 153.

taken and you find that the majority of the people polled were opposed to our involvement. You infer that the majority of people in the United States are opposed to war. For each of the following points explain why the above argument is strengthened, weakened, or is not affected.

1. The survey was conducted by telephone.

2. The survey was based on a stratified random sample where the different subclasses consisted of the main geographical areas in the United States.

3. The survey was conducted by people whose last name was less than ten letters long.

4. The sample consisted of two million people.

C. The report of the Commission on Obscenity and Pornography concluded that there is no causal connection between reading pornographic materials and sex crimes. It recommended the repeal of pornography laws for adults. Does this reflect the attitude of the majority of Americans? A survey is taken and a majority of the people in the survey disagree with the findings of the Commission. It is inferred that the majority of Americans disagree with the conclusions of the Commission. For each of the following points explain why the above argument is strengthened, weakened, or is not affected.

1. The survey was conducted in Chicago, New York City, Philadelphia, and Los Angeles.

2. The survey was conducted in a large number of states spread throughout the United States. It was conducted primarily in the lower socioeconomic section of cities in these states.

3. The survey was conducted by the police.

4. The survey was sponsored by the federal government at a cost of two million dollars.

5. The survey was based on a large stratified random sample where the different subclasses consisted of the Catholic, Jewish, and Protestant faiths.

6. The survey was based on a large stratified random sample

where the different subclasses consisted of the lower, middle, and upper classes.

Answers to Selected Exercises

A.

1. The sample is of sufficient size and since it was a random sample there is a good chance that it is representative of the population. The argument is thus inductively strong.

3. Since Terman's sample was composed basically of children living in California, it was not a random sample. Nevertheless we have reasons for thinking a sample of children from other states would be similar. Furthermore it was a larger sample for the type of testing involved than is usual in such psychological studies. One criticism of the study is that the sample was composed mainly of people with IQ's between 140 and 170. Terman's conclusion is not completely true for people with IQ's higher than 170. However if we restrict Terman's conclusion to people with IQ's between 140 and 170, then his studies do make his conclusion probable.

5. Although many people accept Miss Effron's conclusion, her study does not adequately support it. First of all the sample is fairly small considering the amount of television news coverage. A much larger sample is required. Second, the sampling procedure is likely to make the sample unrepresentative of news broadcasting in general. News shows during a presidential campaign may not be as objective as they are at other times.

B.

1. The sample is restricted to those having telephones so it may be biased. The argument is thus weakened.

3. The argument is not affected since there is no reason to think that the sampling procedure would produce an unrepresentative sample.

C.

1. Nothing is said about the size of the sample and the exact sampling procedure involved. There is little reason for thinking the

cities mentioned would be representative of the rest of the United States. Since there is a high crime rate in these cities, the sample might very well be biased. The argument is thus weakened.

3. Again nothing is stated about the size of the sample and the exact sampling procedure. Unless further information is given, there is little reason for thinking that having the police conduct the survey would make it any more biased or unbiased; hence the argument is not affected.

5. This strengthens the argument. There are more Protestants than Catholics in the United States and there are more Catholics than Jews. Furthermore there is reason to expect a correlation between religious affiliation and one's attitude toward pornography.

3-3 Statistical Syllogism

Another common type of inductive argument is the *statistical syllogism.* Imagine that close to 100 percent of the people who have a streptococcus infection and who are given large doses of penicillin recover from the infection. Imagine also that Jones has such an infection and has been given large doses of penicillin. Then it is very probable that Jones will recover. Stated in standard form, the argument is:

> (1) Close to 100 percent of the people who have a streptococcus infection and who are given large doses of penicillin recover.
> (2) Jones has a streptococcus infection and has been given large doses of penicillin. (make highly probable)
>
> ∴ (3) Jones will recover.

A statistical syllogism has the form:

> (1) X percent of the members of the class S have the property P.
> (2) x is a member of the class S. (   )
>
> ∴ (3) x has the property P.

Often such an argument is not expressed in numerical terms. Instead of stating the first premise in terms of the numerical expression "X percent," it might be expressed by stating that almost all (most, a large proportion) of the members of the class S have the property P. Another way to express the first premise is by stating that there is a high probability that a member of the class S has the property P.

If the first premise states that all or 100 percent of the members of S have P, the argument is no longer inductive but is a deductively valid argument. It has the form:

>   (1)   All (100 percent) of the members of the
>   class S have the property P.
>   (2) x is a member of the class S.
> _____
>   ∴ (3) x has the property P.

Any argument of this form is deductively valid. If the first premise states that almost all or close to 100 percent of the members of S have P, the argument is a statistical syllogism and is not deductively valid.

The closer the value of X is to 100 the greater the inductive strength of the argument. Thus the argument

>   (1)   Close to all Americans want less United
>   States involvement in international affairs.
>   (2)   Jones is an American.(make highly probable)
> _____
>   ∴ (3)   Jones wants less United States involvement
>   in international affairs.

is inductively stronger than the argument below.

>   (1)   60 percent of Americans want less United
>   States involvement in international affairs.
>   (2)   Jones is an American.(make somewhat probable)
> _____
>   ∴ (3)   Jones wants less United States involvement
>   in international affairs.

If the value of X is 50 percent or less, then the argument is not inductively strong. The premises do not make the conclusion probable. If only 50 percent or less of the members of S have P, then if x is a member of S, there is an equal if not greater chance that x does not have P. Thus the premises would not make the conclusion that x has P probable. However if the value of X is greater than 50 percent and less than 100 percent (or the equivalent in nonnumerical terms), then the argument is inductively strong, provided that one further condition is satisfied.

To see what this further condition is, consider the following two arguments:

> (1) Close to 100 percent of the people who have a streptococcus infection and who are given large doses of penicillin recover.
> (2) Jones has a streptococcus infection and has been given large doses of penicillin. (make highly probable)

∴ (3) Jones will recover.

> (1) Close to 100 percent of the people with a streptococcus infection who are given large doses of penicillin and who are very allergic to penicillin do not recover.
> (2) Jones has a streptococcus infection, has been given large doses of penicillin, and is very allergic to penicillin.(make highly probable)

∴ (3) Jones will not recover.

The premises of both arguments might very well be true and they support the conclusions. But the conclusions are inconsistent with one another. They cannot both be true. This situation cannot arise in the case of deductively valid arguments. If an argument is valid and has true premises, then its conclusion must be true. Thus if two arguments are valid and have true premises, the conclusions of both arguments would be true. Hence we cannot have two arguments that are deductively valid with inconsistent conclusions where both sets of premises are true. The problem with the above statistical syllogisms is that the first argument omits information that is relevant to Jones's recovering. The first argument omits the fact that Jones is very allergic to penicillin. This is relevant to whether or not he will recover. x may be a member of a number of different classes that are all relevant to having the property P. If x belongs to the class S_1, there may be a high probability relative to that class that x has the property P. If x belongs to another class S_2, there may be a low probability relative to S_2 that x has P. When considering whether x has P, relevant information that is available should not be omitted. Hence in specifying the class to which x belongs we must not neglect available information that would affect the probability of x's having P. In order for a statistical syllogism to be inductively strong, the following requirements must be satisfied:

(1) The value of X must be greater than 50 percent and less than 100 percent (or the equivalent in nonnumerical terms).

(2) The specification of the class to which x belongs must not omit available information that would be relevant to x's having P.

The first of our above two statistical syllogisms satisfies (1) but fails to satisfy (2). The second argument satisfies them both. Thus only the second argument is inductively strong.

The second requirement follows from a much broader one. In constructing and evaluating inductive arguments, all the known relevant information should be taken into account. This is the *requirement of total relevant information.* We may not know all the information that is relevant; obviously then we cannot take this information into account. But if there is relevant information that is known, we should take this into account when considering inductive arguments.

This requirement also must be satisfied by inductive generalizations. Suppose we take a large random sample of a particular engine part produced by a certain machine and we find that 5 percent of the parts in the sample are defective. If this is all the relevant information that we have, we may infer that approximately 5 percent of the parts produced by this machine are defective. But imagine that we have the further information that previous tests indicated that approximately 10 percent of the parts were defective. Obviously we are now not justified in making the original inference. Additional evidence may affect the inductive strength of an inductive generalization. For an inductive generalization to be inductively strong, we must not omit any available information that affects the probability of whether X percent of the members of the class S have the property P.

It is difficult to specify exactly when information E is relevant to some event or situation A. In general we can say that if E would affect the probability of A, then E is relevant to A. But at present we do not have a more precise characterization of the notion of relevance. Suppose you go out to start your car and it will not start. What things are relevant to its not starting? By past experience we know that the color of the car, the number of doors it has, the size of its tires, and the day of the week are not relevant. The number of doors does not affect the probability that the car will start. Things that are relevant are: the age of the battery, whether there is an adequate supply of gas, the temperature, the timing of the engine, and so on. These things do affect the probability that the car will start. Some authors explain the notion of relevance in terms of causality. Circumstance A is relevant to B if A has a causal effect on B. For instance, a depleted battery causally affects a car's starting ability, so it is relevant. Since there is no causal relation at all between the color of a car and its starting ability, color is not relevant.

The concept of causality is certainly an important part of the notion of relevance. But it is doubtful that we can adequately explain the notion of relevance simply in terms of cause and effect. There may be a high correlation between events A and B and yet A may not causally affect B. Since there is a high correlation, the presence of A affects the probability of B. For example there is a high correlation between wearing a size 38 regular suit and being between five feet six inches and six feet tall. If we know that a man wears a size 38 regular suit, we can predict with reasonable assurance that he is between five feet six inches and six feet tall. But wearing that size suit does not causally affect a man's height.[10]

One way to justify the first premise of a statistical syllogism is to appeal to an inductive generalization. To justify the premise that close to all Americans want less United States involvement in

---

10. For further discussion of the concept of causality see pp. 92-93. For further discussion of the statistical syllogism and the requirement of total relevant information see Hempel, *Aspects of Scientific Explanation*, pp. 53-79, 381-403.

international affairs, it might be argued that a very large stratified random sample of Americans revealed that close to all members of the sample favored less United States involvement. Hence it is probable that close to all Americans favor less involvement. This conclusion then can be used as a premise in our statistical syllogism. If both argument forms are combined, the result is:

(1) X percent of the observed members of the class S have the property P.
∴ (2) X percent of the members of S have P.
(3) x is a member of S.

∴ (4) x has P.

Exercises

A. We are attempting to determine whether x has P. Specify the class to which x belongs without omitting information that would be relevant to x's having P and without including irrelevant information.

1. We want to know whether Jones is going to be drafted and we know that he has a low lottery number, has taken his physical exam and passed, has blue eyes, and has applied to be classified as a conscientious objector.

2. Will Jones do well on his examination in mathematics? He is very bright. However he has just broken up with his fiancée and is very upset over it. Furthermore his grandfather is dead.

3. Will Jones die before he is sixty-five? He has emphysema, is six feet tall, and smokes two or more packs of cigarettes a day.

4. Is Jones going to be the next senator? He is young, aggressive, wealthy, married, plays a little golf, and was an undergraduate liberal arts major.

5. Will Jones show superior achievement? He is the firstborn offspring in his family, is tall, and is an American Protestant.

B. Put the following arguments into argument form. Are they inductively strong or weak?

1. There is a high probability that the children of women who have used drugs such as LSD during pregnancy will suffer birth defects. I pity poor Jane's baby. She regularly uses LSD and she is pregnant.

2. Repeated studies show that most people who have very unhappy childhoods do not have happy marriages. Jones's marriage is probably not very happy since he had a very unhappy childhood.

3. Of a large class of people tested that were thirty-five years of age, it was found that if they smoked two or more packs of cigarettes a day, approximately 40 percent of those tested died before the age of sixty-five. The percentage of nonsmokers who died before age sixty-five was approximately 20 percent. It is probable then that approximately 40 percent of the people who are thirty-five years old and smoke two or more packs of cigarettes a day will die before age sixty-five. Since Jones is thirty-five years old and smokes three packs of cigarettes a day, it is highly probable that he will die before he reaches the age of sixty-five.

4. Studies indicate that at least one-third of urban marriages occur between people who grew up within six city blocks of one another. Joe and Sue had an urban marriage, so they probably grew up within six city blocks of one another.

Answers to Selected Exercises

A.

1. *S:* people who have low lottery numbers, have taken their physicals and passed, and have applied to be classified as conscientious objectors.

3. *S:* people who have emphysema and smoke two or more packs of cigarettes a day.

5. This is a surprising example. Studies indicate that firstborn offspring show superior achievement. They have great representation in *Who's Who*, a number of the highest ranked United States presidents have been firstborn, and a recent survey of finalists for National Merit Scholarships showed that close to 60 percent of them were firstborn. These facts are startling when one considers

that firstborns are outnumbered by later-borns two to one in the United States. To explain the superior achievement it is noted that firstborn children usually get more parental attention, are more responsible and serious minded, and are more oriented toward adult standards.[11] It also has been shown that there is a fairly high correlation between being tall (approximately six feet to six feet five inches) and achieving a higher status occupation. For example, bishops tend to be taller than small town ministers, university presidents tend to be taller than college presidents, and railroad presidents tend to be taller than railroad station agents.[12] Finally studies also indicate that Protestants in our society tend to hold higher ranked positions than Catholics.[13] The class S is thus

> $S:$ people who are firstborn offspring who are tall and who also are American Protestants.

B.

1.   (1) There is a high probability that children of women who have used such drugs as LSD during pregnancy will suffer birth defects.

     (2) Jane is a woman who has used LSD during pregnancy.(make highly probable)

     ∴ (3) Jane's baby will have birth defects.

Assuming that the requirement of total relevant information is satisfied, this argument is inductively strong.

3.   (1) Approximately 40 percent of the people tested that were thirty-five years of age and who smoked two or more packs of cigarettes a day died before the age of sixty-five.

     ∴ (2) Approximately 40 percent of the people who are thirty-five years of age and smoke two or more packs of cigarettes a day will die before the age of sixty-five.

---

11. See Johnson and Medinnus, *Child Psychology,* pp. 257-64.
12. Elton B. McNeil, *Human Socialization* (Belmont, Calif.: Brooks Cole, 1969), p. 125.
13. Elizabeth B. Hurlock, *Developmental Psychology* (New York: McGraw-Hill, 1968), p. 610.

> (3)   Jones is thirty-five years old and smokes three packs of cigarettes a day.(make highly probable)

∴ (4)   Jones will die before he reaches the age of sixty-five.

This argument is inductively weak since the percentage of people who are thirty-five, smoke two or more packs a day, and die before age sixty-five is less than 50 percent.

3-4 Analogical Arguments

A third common type of inductive argument is the *analogical argument* or *argument by analogy.* If Jones infers that the car he just purchased will get approximately eighteen miles per gallon of gas since it is just like the past three cars he owned and they all got approximately eighteen miles per gallon of gas, then his reasoning would be based on the analogy or similarity between the new car and the three previous cars. The cars may be similar in that they are all brand B and model M, have eight cylinders with the same cubic capacity, have the same carburetion system, and will be driven under similar conditions by the same driver. The principle upon which an analogical argument is based is: Since objects O_1, $O_2, \ldots, O_n$ are similar in certain respects, they can be expected to be similar in certain other respects. The logical form of the argument is:

> (1)   Objects $O_1, O_2, \ldots, O_n$ have properties P_2, $P_3, \ldots, P_j$ in common.
> (2)   Objects $O_2, O_3, \ldots, O_n$ have property P_1 in common. (   )

∴ (3)   Object O_1 has property P_1.

If we let

> O_1: Car just purchased
> O_2: Car owned prior to O_1
> O_3: Car owned prior to O_2

O_4 : Car owned prior to O_3
P_1 : Gets approximately eighteen miles per gallon of gas
P_2 : Brand B
P_3 : Model M
P_4 : Eight cylinders with the same cubic capacity
P_5 : Carburetion system C
P_6 : Driven under similar conditions by same driver

then our example can be symbolized as:

(1) Objects O_1, O_2, O_3, and O_4 have properties
     P_2, P_3, P_4, P_5, and P_6 in common.
(2) Objects O_2, O_3, and O_4 also have property
     P_1 in common. (make highly probable)

∴ (3) Object O_1 has property P_1.

In order for an argument by analogy to be inductively strong, a number of nonformal conditions must be satisfied. The most important of these conditions is that the properties by virtue of which the objects O_1, O_2, . . . , O_n are similar must be *relevant* to object O_1 having the property P_1. Suppose it is argued that Jones is probably six feet tall since Jones is a lot like Smith in that they both are good looking, have good singing voices, belong to the same fraternity, have the same hair color, and furthermore Smith is six feet tall. Even though they share a number of properties, these properties are not relevant to Jones's being six feet tall. A few properties that would be relevant are: height of the parents, national origin, and suit size. Unless the common properties are relevant to the inferred property, the argument is worthless.

Another condition that must be considered is the number of relevant properties held in common and the number of relevant properties not held in common. To use the car example again, imagine that the new car is similar to the previous ones only in that they are all the same brand and model. Since the new car has only these two relevant properties in common with the previous cars, the basis of the analogy is weaker. Hence the argument is inductively weaker. There also would be a number of relevant properties that were not held in common, namely, P_4 through P_6. Since there are these relative differences or disanalogies, the analogy is weaker. Again the argument is made inductively weaker. In general, the fewer the number of relevant properties held in common, the less probable the conclusion is; and the greater the number of relevant properties not held in common, the less probable the conclusion is. Thus if O_1 and the set of objects O_2, $O_3, \ldots, O_n$ have only a few relevant properties in common, the conclusion is less probable than it would be if they shared a greater number of relevant properties. If O_1 and the set of objects $O_2, O_3, \ldots, O_n$ exhibit a great number of relevant dissimilarities, the conclusion is less probable than it would be if the relevant dissimilarities were fewer in number.

A further condition that should be taken into account is the number of objects included in $O_2, \ldots, O_n$ that have the properties $P_1, \ldots, P_j$. Usually the fewer the number of objects included in $O_2, \ldots, O_n$ that have $P_1, \ldots, P_j$, the weaker the argument. Assume that Jones had only one previous car with the properties $P_1, \ldots, P_4$ and he inferred that since his new car has P_2, P_3, and P_4, it will probably have P_1. This argument would be weaker than the original argument when the number of objects that had $P_1, \ldots, P_4$ was greater.

Another condition that should be considered is the number of objects with $P_2, \ldots, P_j$ that lack P_1. The greater the number of such objects, the weaker the argument. For example, if Jones discovered through an examination of the dealer's records that 60 percent of the cars with $P_2, \ldots, P_4$ lack P_1, then his argument becomes worthless.

In general it can be said that in order for an analogical argument to be inductively strong, the properties $P_2, \ldots, P_j$ must be relevant to the inferred property P_1, and:

(1)   The greater the number of relevant properties held in common, the stronger the argument.

(2)   The fewer the number of relevant dissimilarities, the stronger the argument.

(3)   The greater the number of objects included in $O_2, \ldots, O_n$ that have $P_1, \ldots, P_j$, the stronger the argument.

(4)   The fewer the number of objects with $P_2, \ldots, P_j$ that lack P_1, the stronger the argument.

As is the case with any inductive argument the requirement of total relevant information must be satisfied. Known relevant information should not be neglected when constructing or evaluating an inductive argument. In attempting to determine whether the properties $P_2, \ldots, P_j$ are relevant to P_1, we must appeal to our total relevant information. Conditions (1) through (4) also are determined on the basis of our total relevant information.

Analogical reasoning is quite frequent in science. An interesting example is Elie Metchnikoff's attempt to find a means of preventing syphillis. Metchnikoff developed an ointment he thought would prevent the disease. He inoculated apes, monkeys, and chimpanzees with the disease by scratching the virus into their skins. When the ointment was rubbed into the scratch, the animal did not develop the disease. Metchnikoff then reasoned that there were a great number of physiological similarities between apes, chimpanzees, monkeys, and man. These common physiological features were relevant to contracting diseases. Furthermore there were no known relevant features that such animals had that men did not have or vice versa that would affect whether the ointment would work. Nor did Metchnikoff know of any creatures that possessed the same physiological properties and yet were not protected by the ointment. Since he had tested the ointment on a great number of monkeys, apes, and chimpanzees and had found it to be successful, he concluded that it was probable that it also would protect man. He then induced a young medical student by the name of Maisonneuve to volunteer to be inoculated with syphillis. Metchnikoff inoculated a chimpanzee, a monkey, and Maisonneuve. Then he applied the ointment to the student. The chimpanzee and monkey contracted the disease but the medical student did not.[14]

A similar example is Paul Ehrlich's attempt to use a form of arsenic to cure a man of syphillis. Ehrlich developed a chemical compound that would cure animals of the disease. He tested it on such creatures as chickens, rabbits, and mice. Would it cure humans? He reasoned that since his test animals and humans shared so many relevant physiological features, it would probably work for humans too. The analogy involved here is weaker than in the Metchnikoff example. There was an important relevant dissimilarity that Ehrlich noted. A chemical compound involving a lethal substance such as arsenic may not harm an animal if given a small dose, whereas the same dose might kill a man. This dissimilarity weakens the analogy.[15]

---

14. See Paul de Kruif, *Microbe Hunters* (New York: Harcourt, Brace, 1926), chap. vii.
15. Ibid., chap. xxi.

Exercises

A. Explain why each of the following analogical arguments is inductively strong or why it is not.

1. Robert Tryon's experiments with breeding rats makes it probable that selective breeding (eugenics) affects intelligence in rats.[16] What we know about heredity indicates that rats and humans share a number of hereditary principles. Thus it seems probable that eugenics would affect intelligence in humans too.

2. Martin Luther King's acts of civil disobedience were morally justified. Since our act of taking over the administration building is a public and nonviolent protest intended to alter a law that we take to be immoral, our action too is morally justified.

3. Regularly taking LSD has great adverse physical effects. Since marijuana is a hallucinogen like LSD, it too probably produces great adverse physical effects.

4. Extensive studies indicate that affection for the mother in young rhesus monkeys depends in large part on close bodily contact. Baby rhesus monkeys were taken from their mothers and were given a soft cloth substitute mother and a wire substitute mother. The infant monkeys spent most of their time clinging to the soft cloth monkey. When the monkeys were confronted with a strange object that frightened them, they would rush to the soft cloth mother rubbing their bodies against hers. Then they would venture out to investigate the object after their fears had been reduced. When a monkey was placed in a large strange room without its soft mother, it would huddle in the corner. When its mother was there it would cling to her for a while and then venture out returning every once in a while. Human children exhibit the same type of behavior and their general patterns of development are the same. Thus it is probable that affection for the mother in humans also depends in large part on close bodily contact.[17]

5. Capital punishment is similar to a citizen of the state killing another person. Since the latter is wrong so is the former.

---

16. Cox, *Psychology*, p. 191.
17. Harry F. Harlow, "Love in Infant Monkeys," *Scientific American* 200 (June 1959): 68-74.

6. If a person makes a contract and then violates it, he forfeits all the claims granted to him in the contract. Being a member of a democracy is similar to making a contract with the other members of society to work for the benefit of all. Thus if one breaks the rules of society, he relinquishes all claims to the rights given to him by society.

B. You know that equal power in policy formation for students at university A was beneficial to the university. You infer that since your university is similar to university A, such power would have the same result at your university. For each of the following points explain why the above argument is strengthened, weakened, or is not affected.

1. The student population at university A and at your university is very similar with respect to social and economic background.

2. A number of universities that are similar to university A gave the students equal power in policy formation and it was not beneficial to the university.

3. There are more female students at your university than at university A.

4. Universities B and C, which are quite similar to university A and to your university, had the same favorable results when students were given such power.

5. The average age of a student at university A is 20.4 while the average age at your university is 18.7.

6. The majority of the students at university A are highly motivated whereas most of the students at your university are fairly apathetic.

C. A democratic form of government for country A has maximized the welfare of the people in A. Country B is similar to A. Thus it is probable that a democratic form of government for country B will maximize the welfare of the people of B. For each of the following points, explain why the above argument is strengthened, weakened, or is not affected.

1. There is strong national allegiance in both countries.

2. Less than 1 percent of the people of country A are illiterate but a high percentage of the people of country B are illiterate.

3. The average age of the people of country B is 35.9 and it is 46.3 in country A.

4. The standard of living of country A is high while the standard of living of country B is low.

Answers to Selected Exercises

A.

1. This argument is inductively strong. The mechanism of heredity is basically the same for all animals including man. Thus rats and men share a number of properties relevant to the inferred property. Given what we know about heredity, it appears as if there are few if any relevant dissimilarities. Since a large number of rats were tested and we know of no animals that share the same heredity principles and yet lack the inferred property, the conclusion of the argument is probable.

3. The argument is inductively weak. The only common property mentioned is that LSD and marijuana are both hallucinogens. There are relevant dissimilarities too. LSD is much more potent than marijuana. Thus the argument as it stands is weak.

5. This argument is inductively weak. Capital punishment and an individual's killing another person are similar in that they both involve the taking of a human life. There are, however, a number of relevant dissimilarities. The case of capital punishment involves a long process of trial by jury to see if the person is guilty of a major crime. If the person is guilty of such a crime, then capital punishment is inflicted. It may be inflicted on the guilty person to punish him, to protect society, or to deter others from committing the same type of crime.

B.

1. The argument is strengthened since the analogy is made stronger.

3. The argument is not affected since the property is not relevant to the inferred property.

5. It is weakened since the analogy is made weaker. Maturity would be a relevant dissimilarity.

C.

1. The argument is strengthened since the analogy is made stronger.

3. It is not affected since the property is irrelevant to the inferred property.

3-5 Common Fallacies

An argument is fallacious if the premises do not adequately support the conclusion. If we isolate a number of types of fallacious arguments, it will help us to avoid relying on them. The fallacies of affirming the consequent, denying the antecedent, biased sample, and insufficient sample size have already been discussed. A few more common fallacies are discussed below.

One very common fallacy is the *ad hominem* argument. Literally this means "argument directed to the man." Imagine that Jones, an ex-convict, runs for a political office and argues that there is a drastic need for welfare reform. His opponent Smith might argue as follows:

> Jones maintains that there is a need to overhaul the welfare system. Now this man is an ex-convict, a common criminal. Can we trust the word of such a man? I suggest that we cannot. I therefore urge you not to vote for a change in the present welfare system.

Here Smith rejects the claim that there is a need to reform the welfare system not by examining the available evidence but by attacking Jones's *character*. This personal attack is not logically relevant to whether there is a need to alter the present welfare system. Thus Smith has not adequately supported his rejection of Jones's claim and hence his argument is fallacious.

Consider a slightly different case. Jones proposes that out-of-state students who reach the age of twenty-one be classified as residents of the state. Smith in turn argues:

Jones suggests that out-of-state students who reach the age of twenty-one be classified as residents of the state. Now why does Jones suggest this? Well, he happens to be an out-of-state student who just became twenty-one. Certainly *he* would be for the proposal.

The implication of Smith's argument is that the proposal should be rejected. What Smith has done is to attack the proposal on the basis of Jones's *interests*. The fact that Jones would benefit if the proposal were accepted may lead us to question his motives. Nevertheless the fact that the proposal is in his interests is logically irrelevant to whether or not the proposal is a good one. Thus Smith's argument is again fallacious.

Another example of the ad hominem fallacy is this case. Jones argues that women must be given equality and Smith responds by arguing:

Jones says that women must be given equality. Well look who is talking. We all know that Jones himself hires women only for secretarial positions, that he never promotes them, and pays them less than men.

Instead of examining the merits of Jones's claim, Smith has attacked Jones personally. Smith may have shown that Jones's actions are inconsistent with his belief that women must be given equality, but this again is logically irrelevant to the truth of the claim.

There are other types of examples of the ad hominem fallacy. The types we have considered have the following logical form:

(1) Person A asserts that p.
(2) Person B rejects p by attacking A personally (his character, interests, special circumstances) where the personal attack is logically irrelevant to the truth of p.

Sometimes attacking the person who makes a claim is logically relevant to the truth or falsity of the claim. If Jones asserts that he is a good candidate for membership on the Supreme Court, the fact that he is a known racketeer gives us good reason for thinking he would not make a good judge. In this case attacking Jones's character is logically relevant to his claim. If a person claims to know that p, one way to attack his claim is to argue that he is not in a position to know. Such an attack is logically relevant to his claim. If attacking the person is logically relevant to the truth or falsity of the claim made, then it does not follow that rejecting the claim on the basis of such an attack is fallacious. Rejecting the claim on the basis of a personal attack is fallacious only when such an attack is logically irrelevant to the truth or falsity of what is asserted.

Another common fallacy is *misuse of authority*. Frequently we appeal to authorities when considering the truth or falsity of some statement. Such appeals, however, can be misused. If Jones argues that God must be all-powerful since Einstein, the great physicist, said that in creating the universe God revealed his omnipotence, then Jones is appealing to an authority to support his claim that God is all-powerful. His argument has the form:

> (1) A is an authority and asserts that p. (makes probable)
>
> ---
>
> $\therefore$ (2) p.

This argument form is fallacious as it stands. Unless A is an authority on the subject matter of p, the fact that A asserts that p gives us little if any reason for thinking that p is true. Einstein was an authority in the area of physics but he was not an authority on God. Thus Jones's argument is fallacious.

An authority in a certain area is reliable if his assertions about that area are correct most of the time. If a reliable authority on the subject matter of p honestly asserts that p is true on the basis of the total relevant evidence available, this gives us reason for thinking that p is true. If there are no other reliable authorities concerning p that honestly assert that p is false on the basis of the total relevant evidence available, then we are justified in accepting that p is true. Arguments of the form

> (1) A is a reliable authority on the subject matter of p, and, on the basis of the total relevant evidence available, honestly asserts that p is true.
>
> (2)   There is no reliable authority concerning p that honestly asserts on the basis of the

total relevant evidence available that p is false.(make probable)

$\therefore$ (3) p.

A common fallacy involving causal relations is the post hoc fallacy.[18] Knowledge of causal relations plays an important part in our reasoning. If our car will not start we seek the cause. Perhaps the battery is not sufficiently charged or there is no gas. In this example we infer the cause on the basis of observed effects. At other times we infer the effect from the cause. Such causal knowledge enables us to make inferences about the future and about the past. If we know that smoking two or more packs of cigarettes a day causes emphysema, then we can predict that Jones *will* get the disease if he smokes two or more packs a day. Given our present causal knowledge about physics, we can make inferences about what happened in the past that produced our solar system. In order for such causal reasoning to be reliable, obviously the causal relations appealed to must actually hold. If smoking does not cause emphysema, then our inference that Jones will get the disease if he smokes is not reliable.

The post hoc fallacy is the fallacy of concluding that an event E_2 is caused by another event E_1 simply on the basis of the fact that E_2 followed or follows E_1. The fact that E_2 followed or follows E_1 does not adequately support the conclusion that E_2 is caused by E_1. It may just be a matter of coincidence that E_2 follows E_1. For example, imagine that every time Jones goes to take a nap (E_1), the phone rings (E_2). E_2 follows E_1, but it does not follow that E_1 causes E_2. It may be just a matter of coincidence that every time Jones starts to take a nap, the phone rings. No causal relation need exist between the two events.

Sometimes an event E_2 may follow another event E_1 where E_1 does not cause E_2 and yet there is a causal link. Frequently when the barometer indicates falling air pressure (E_1) it rains (E_2). Now E_1 certainly does not cause E_2 and yet the relation between the two events is not merely due to coincidence. The atmospheric conditions that cause E_1 also cause E_2. Here the two events E_1 and E_2 are related to a third event E_3. E_3 causes both E_1 and E_2.

---

18. The name comes from "post hoc ergo propter hoc" which means "after this; therefore, because of this."

The controversy over whether smoking cigarettes causes cancer is a good illustration of the difficulty of establishing a cause and effect relationship. There is a statistical uniformity between the heavy smoking of cigarettes and such diseases as lung cancer, emphysema, and heart ailments. Some people have inferred from this uniformity that smoking causes such diseases. It has been replied however that no one has really shown a direct or indirect causal link between these events. For example it has not been shown that cigarette smoke causes lung cancer in rats.

The conditions under which a causal relation is established are complex. The fact that E_2 follows or usually follows E_1 is relevant to whether such a relation exists, but it does not provide sufficient evidence to conclude that E_1 causes E_2. We also must ask, "Given our total knowledge, is it reasonable to expect a causal relation to hold between E_1 and E_2?" Another question to be asked is, "Is there any other plausible explanation of why the two events are associated?" Our total knowledge gives us good reason for thinking that heredity causally affects such things as intelligence. Thus in the example of the selective breeding of rats, we are justified in concluding that eugenics affects intelligence in rats, since there is no other plausible explanation and our total knowledge makes it reasonable to expect such a connection.[19]

The last common fallacy to be discussed is a fallacy in a special sense. Consider the following argument:

> (1) The only acts for which one should be held morally responsible are those that are voluntary.
>
> ∴ (2) No one should be held morally responsible for involuntary acts.

If we carefully examine what the premise and conclusion assert, we find that they state the same thing. The conclusion expresses exactly what the premise does, only it does so in a slightly different way. Since the conclusion is just a restatement of the premise, the argument *begs the question.* An argument is said to

19. For further discussion on the concept of causality and techniques for establishing causal relations see Irving M. Copi, *Introduction to Logic,* 4th ed. (New York: Macmillan, 1972), chap. 12, and Brian Skyrms, *Choice and Chance* (Belmont, Calif.: Dickenson, 1966), pp. 80-110.

beg the question just in case at least one of the premises is logically equivalent to the conclusion. Notice that an argument that begs the question is deductively valid. If the conclusion is either an explicit or implicit restatement of one of the premises, then it would be impossible for the premises to be true and the conclusion false. Thus an argument that begs the question is not fallacious in the sense that it is not logically correct. It is fallacious in the sense that the question at issue is whether the conclusion is true. If one of the premises is logically equivalent to it, the conclusion is already assumed to be true. Thus the question whether the conclusion is true is begged.[20]

Exercises

A. If there are fallacies in the following arguments, identify them.

1. Dr. Benjamin Spock, the noted pediatrician, has argued that the war in Indochina is corrupt and thus we should not participate in it. We ought to pull out then.

2. Criminals deserve equal rights only if they have not harmed society. Since they have harmed society, they do not deserve equal rights.

3. Student activists have argued that universities are politically oriented institutions and thus they should assert their positions on political questions. A large number of these student leaders have been involved in violence and criminal action. We should not heed the advice of these people.

4. G. E. Moore argued that he could prove that there existed an external world. He said:

> I can prove now, for instance, that two human hands exist. How? By holding up my two hands, and saying, as I make a certain gesture with the right hand, "Here is one hand," and adding, as I make a certain gesture with the left, "and here is another."[21]

20. For a delightful and more comprehensive discussion of common fallacies see Howard Kahane, *Logic and Contemporary Rhetoric* (Belmont, Calif.: Wadsworth, 1971).
21. G. E. Moore, "Proof of an External World," *Philosophical Papers* (London: George Allen and Unwin Ltd., 1959), pp. 145-46.

5. The Pope has declared that the fetus is human life. Hence abortion is wrong since the fetus is human life and it is wrong to take human life.

6. A high percentage of people who regularly smoke marijuana go on to try other drugs such as LSD and heroin. We ought to make marijuana illegal since it leads to using other drugs.

7. The report of the Commission of Obscenity and Pornography must be rejected. It states that there is no causal relation between reading erotic materials and sex crimes. But this is just false. Even President Nixon has rejected the report.

8. Do not pay any attention to the women in the women's liberation movement. Some of them are homosexual radicals and others are frustrated in other ways.

9. No act of violence can be justified unless it benefits the large majority of the people. We must consider the consequences of the act. If it does not benefit the majority it cannot be justified. Thus the only violent acts that can be justified are those that benefit the majority.

10. Smith argues that we should move the dumping center out away from the city. To have it so close to the city could pollute the water supply. It is easy to see why Smith would argue this way. He owns a large farm outside the city that would make a perfect dumping center.

B.

1. Read the editorial page in your local newspaper and find examples of the fallacies discussed in this section.

Answers to Selected Exercises

A.

1. Misuse of authority

3. Ad hominem

5. There may be some disagreement over this argument. The Pope may be an authority on certain religious matters but there is a question as to whether he is an authority on the fetus.

7. The sentence "But this is just false" begs the question and appealing to the president is a misuse of authority.

9. This argument begs the question. The first and last sentences are logically equivalent to one another.

3-6 Summary of Basic Concepts

1. An argument is *inductively strong* just in case (1) it is not deductively valid, and (2) if the premises are true, then the conclusion is probable.

2. The degree of inductive strength of an argument depends on how probable the conclusion is given the truth of the premises. Inductive strength is a matter of degree; validity is not.

3. Inductive strength, unlike validity, is not a formal property. Whether an argument is inductively strong depends on a number of nonformal conditions.

Exercises

1. Why is inductive reasoning important?

2. What are two differences between deductively valid arguments and inductively strong arguments?

3. Distinguish inductive strength from truth.

4. If we are concerned with whether an argument makes a conclusion probable, what two main questions should we ask?

5. What is the difference between a universal and a statistical syllogism?

6. What is a random sample? Give an example.

7. What is a stratified random sample? Give an example.

8. Why are such sampling techniques important?

9. What are the fallacies of insufficient sample size and biased sample? Give examples.

10. What conditions must be satisfied if an inductive generalization is to be inductively strong?

11. What conditions must be satisfied if a statistical syllogism is to be inductively strong? What is the requirement of total relevant information and how does it apply to statistical syllogism?

12. What features must be considered when evaluating the strength of an analogical argument? Explain each feature and why they affect the inductive strength of an analogical argument.

13. Why is an ad hominem argument fallacious?

14. Discuss the conditions under which appealing to an authority supports or does not support a conclusion.

15. Explain the post hoc fallacy.

16. If an argument that begs the question is valid, then why is such an argument worthless?

Language and Argument

4-1 Ambiguity and Vagueness

If we are to be in a position to critically evaluate an argument, we must understand the meaning of the statements in it. Consider the following example:

> (1) If all events are caused, then no man has free will.
> (2) If man has no free will, then man is not morally responsible for his actions.
> (3) All events are caused.
> ───────────────────────────
> ∴ (4) Man is not morally responsible for his actions.

Are the premises true? In order to evaluate the truth of the premises, we must understand the meaning of the terms "event," "cause," "free will," "action," and "moral responsibility." Frequently the meaning of some term in an argument is not clearly understood which makes it difficult to assess the merits of the argument.

A number of features of language often lead to confusion and to a lack of clarity. Ambiguity is one such feature. A quick glance at the dictionary reveals that a very large number of words have more than one meaning. Included among the different meanings of "common" are (1) belonging to or being shared by members of a group, and (2) of ordinary occurrence (familiar, prevalent). Confusion is not usually generated simply because a word has more than one meaning. However, if it cannot be determined from the context which meaning is intended, this may very well create confusion. A word W is said to be *ambiguous* if it has more than one meaning and from the context it cannot be determined which meaning is intended.[1] The word "bank" has more than one meaning but it is not ambiguous as it occurs in the sentence "Jones was swimming and as he climbed out of the water he slipped on the bank." However, in the sentence "The bank was muddy" the word "bank" is ambiguous. The word "common" also is used ambiguously in the sentence "That is a common bicycle." This may create confusion because the sentence could mean that it is an ordinary or prevalent type of bicycle, or it could mean that it is a bicycle shared or owned by a group of people. If a word is used ambiguously, the intended meaning can usually be indicated by some sort of qualification or addition to the sentence. To indicate that it is the first meaning of "common" that is intended, we might say "That is a very prevalent type of bicycle." To indicate that it is the second meaning that is intended, we are required to add something like "That is a common bicycle, that is, we all share it."

The concept of ambiguity can be extended to include whole sentences. A sentence S is *ambiguous* if it has more than one meaning and from the context it cannot be determined which meaning is intended.[2] If we are given the sentences

> Jones deposited his paycheck in the bank. While doing this he noticed that the bank was muddy. He was upset that the bank president would allow the floors of his bank to be so dirty.

we can determine the intended meaning of the sentence "The bank was muddy" by considering it in relation to the other sentences. Hence it is not ambiguous. However in the context

---

1. "Context" in this case refers to the sentence in which W occurs as well as the broader speech context if there is one.
2. "Context" in this case refers to the set of sentences in which S occurs as well as the broader speech context if there is one.

"There were pretty flowers all over. But the bank was muddy" we cannot determine which meaning is intended. Thus in this case "The bank was muddy" is ambiguous.

If a word W is ambiguous, then the sentence S that contains W has more than one meaning. This in itself is not detrimental to clarity as long as we can determine from the context the intended meaning of the sentence. But if the sentence is ambiguous, this may result in confusion. It will not be clear what the intended meaning is. If a sentence in an argument is ambiguous, it may be true under one interpretation and yet false under another. Which is the intended meaning? If we cannot determine which meaning is intended, we cannot determine whether the argument is sound. Thus when constructing or evaluating an argument, one should make sure that the premises and conclusion are not ambiguous. Take the free will argument stated above. The first premise is "If all events are caused, then no man has free will." The expression "free will" as it occurs in the argument is ambiguous. In one sense of the expression, to say that Jones's act was an act of free will is to say that Jones was not coerced by an external agent to do the act. Thus if Jones lies because another man has a gun on him and has ordered him to lie, his act is not one of free will. But if no one threatens or forces Jones to lie, then his act of lying is an act of free will. In this sense of "free will" the first premise is false. Even if certain things caused Jones to come to college, it does not follow that he was coerced by an external agent. If to say that a person's act was an act of free will means that his act was not caused, then in this sense of "free will" the first premise would be true. We cannot determine whether the argument is sound unless we know which meaning of "free will" is intended.

Vagueness is another feature of language that frequently leads to a lack of clarity. An expression is *vague* if there are cases where it cannot be determined whether the expression applies, and this indeterminacy of application is due to the meaning of the expression, not to a lack of evidence. Consider the word "elderly." A person is elderly if he is somewhat old. The word is not ambiguous but it is vague. There are cases where it is not clear whether we should say the person is elderly or not. It is clear that a person who is forty-nine years old is not elderly while a person who is seventy-two is elderly. These cases raise no problems. But how about a person who is sixty-two, sixty-five, sixty-seven, sixty-nine, . . . ? These are cases where we are not sure what we should say. This indeterminacy of application is not due to a lack of evidence about the person. Even if we had all the information available about the person, we might still not know what to say. This case is unlike the case where we do not know whether to say that Jones committed the murder. This indeterminacy would not be due to vagueness but to lack of evidence. Given more information, we could determine whether the expression "committed the murder" applied to Jones. The reason it is not always clear whether we should say that a person is elderly is not that we need more evidence about the person. Neither is it that we do not understand the meaning of the word nor that it is ambiguous. The term is simply vague.

A more interesting example of a vague word is "patriotic." A patriotic person is a person who loves his country and zealously supports its welfare. We understand the meaning of the term, but there certainly are cases where it is not clear whether we should say a person is patriotic or not. Again the indeterminacy of application is not due to lack of evidence. The term is simply vague. Some other vague words are "happy," "university," "love," "war."

Some words are both vague and ambiguous. If we assert that Jones is mature, this is ambiguous. It could mean he is intellectually, emotionally, or physically mature. If we qualify the sentence to read "Jones is emotionally mature" the intended meaning becomes clear, but the expression "emotionally mature" is vague. To be emotionally mature is to be fully developed emotionally so that the person is emotionally well adjusted. But can we always determine whether to call a person emotionally mature even if we know the person very well? Some cases will arise where we are not sure whether to apply the term, and this will not be due to the fact that the evidence is incomplete.

Sometimes vagueness is confused with the lack of being specific. If Smith asks where Jones is going and he receives the reply "Somewhere along the East Coast," Smith might complain that this is awfully vague. The problem of indeterminacy in this case is due basically to the lack of the speaker's being more specific. This is not to deny that the expression "along the East Coast" is somewhat vague. There may be cases where it is not definite whether we should say that the location is along the East Coast. How close to the coast does it have to be? Even though this expression is somewhat vague, the indeterminacy of the reply is due basically to the lack of the speaker's providing more specific information such as "He is going to Boston."

If an expression in a statement is vague, it may cause difficulties when we attempt to evaluate the truth or falsity of that statement. Take the assertion that all wars are morally wrong. The word "war" is vague. The violence and force directed against Japan during World War II is a clear case of war. In other cases it is more difficult to know what to say. Imagine that during the Cuban missile crisis the United States had invaded Cuba and destroyed the missiles. Suppose the fighting lasted four days. It is not clear that this should be called a war. This indeterminacy of application makes it difficult to assess the truth of the claim that all wars are morally wrong. There may be examples where the action taken against another politically organized body is not wrong and yet it is not clear whether we should call this action an instance of war. In this case we would not know if the original claim were true or false. It is difficult to avoid being vague altogether, but when constructing and evaluating arguments we should be alert to the problem.[3]

Exercises

1. Does the word "prostitute" have more than one meaning? Is the word ambiguous as it is used in the following sentence "She was a prostitute"? Is "prostitute" vague?

2. Does the word "subjective" have more than one meaning? Is it ambiguous as it occurs in the sentence "The grading was subjective"? Is the expression vague?

3. Does the word "alienated" have more than one meaning? Is the word ambiguous as it is used in the sentence "She was alienated from the group"? Is "alienate" vague?

4. What *exactly* is being asserted in the following sentences?

The course was not relevant.
Ethical judgments are subjective.

---

3. For an excellent and more extended discussion of vagueness see William P. Alston, *Philosophy of Language* (Englewood Cliffs, N. J.: Prentice-Hall, 1964), chap. v.

Ethical judgments are relative.
Jones is a good teacher.

Answers to Selected Exercises

1. "Prostitute" is defined as meaning (a) to submit to promiscuous lewdness especially for hire, and (b) to devote to base or unworthy purposes (to prostitute one's talents). Even though it has more than one meaning, it is not used ambiguously in the sentence "She was a prostitute." Both (a) and (b) are vague.

3. The word "alienated" can be used to refer either to (a) being *physically* cut off from an individual group, or (b) being *psychologically* cut off from an individual or group. It is not clear from the context of the sentence which meaning is intended. (b) is clearly vague, and there also may be cases where it is not clear whether a person is physically cut off from an individual or group.

4-2 Definition

One important way to explain or specify the meaning of an expression is to give a definition of it. For example we might define the term "father" as meaning *a male parent.* What is being defined is the *expression.* To indicate that we are talking about the expression, quotation marks are placed around it. Thus the sentence

"father" means *a male parent*

should be read as: the word "father" means *a male parent.* The sentence "Boston has six letters" is misleading. The city of Boston does not have six letters; the word does. To indicate we are referring to the name of the city and not to the city, we again place quotation marks around the word. Thus the sentence should be: "Boston" has six letters. The expression to be defined is called the *definiendum* and the defining expression is called the *definiens.* The entire expression "father" means *a male parent*

is called an *explicit definition.*

When giving explicit definitions we have to be careful to avoid circularity. An explicit definition is *circular* just in case the definiendum or a grammatical variant of the definiendum occurs in the definiens in such a way that one cannot understand the definiens unless one already understands the definiendum. Suppose we defined "a person who is a parent" as *a person who is male or female and is a parent.* This would be a circular definition since a grammatical variant of the definiendum occurs in the definiens in such a way that one cannot understand the definiens unless one already understands the definiendum.

Sometimes a series of definitions is circular. Consider the following definitions:

(1) "parent" means *person who is a father or mother.*
(2) "father" means *male parent.*
(3) "mother" means *female parent.*

In definition (1) the term "parent" does not occur in the definiens. But in order to understand definition (1), the definitions (2) and (3) must be understood. In these definitions the term "parent" does occur. Hence in order to comprehend definitions (2) and (3), we must already understand the first definition. Thus the series of definitions is circular. The following series is not circular:

(1) "parent" means *person who is a father or mother.*
(2) "father" means *male person who has a son or daughter.*
(3) "mother" means *female person who has a son or daughter.*

Sometimes a definition appears circular when it is not. Take the definition:

"teacher" means *person who teaches.*

A grammatical variant of the definiendum occurs in the definiens. But it does not follow that the definition is circular. If we can understand the definiens without already having to understand the definiendum, the definition will not be circular. We can define "person who teaches" as *a person who imparts knowledge so that others may learn.* Given this definition, the definiens of the definition of "teacher" can be understood without already understanding the meaning of the word "teacher." Hence the definition is not circular.

There are a number of different types of explicit definitions. Three important ones are *reportive, stipulative,* and *reconstructive* definitions. A reportive definition is intended to report the ordinary or established meaning of an expression. A correct reportive definition of the word "father" as it applies to humans would be:

"father" means *a male person who has a son or daughter.*

If we are concerned with the sense of "brother" that implies having common parents and not the sense in which all men are said to be brothers, then

"brother" means *male sibling*

is another example of a correct reportive definition.

A reportive definition is correct only if the definiendum means the same as the definiens. Now if two expressions W_1 and W_2 have the same meaning, then whenever one of the expressions correctly applies to something, it follows that the other expression will correctly apply to that thing also. It would be impossible for either W_1 or W_2 to correctly apply to something to which the other expression did not also correctly apply. Thus if a reportive definition is correct, it is impossible for either the definiendum to correctly apply to something to which the definiens does not apply, or for the definiens to correctly apply to something to which the definiendum does not apply. The above definition of "brother" is correct so if someone is a brother it follows that he is a male sibling and if someone is a male sibling it follows that he is a brother.

To test whether a reportive definition is correct, we try to describe a possible situation where the definiendum correctly applies but the definiens does not, or where the definiens correctly applies but the definiendum does not. The example does not have to be something that has actually happened or will ever happen. But it does have to be something that could possibly happen. If we can produce such an example, it follows that the definition is not correct. Such an example is a counterexample to the definition. The method of testing a reportive definition is the *method of counterexample*. If we cannot produce a counterexample, it does not follow that the definition is correct. Counterexamples may exist; perhaps we just have not thought of them. Nevertheless not being able to produce a counterexample does give us some reason for thinking the definition is correct. Hence if we cannot produce a counterexample, we can tentatively accept the definition as correct.

Let us take an example. Suppose "bachelor" were defined as *a male person who is not married.* Would this be a correct reportive definition?[4] Can we produce a counterexample to the definition? No example can be produced where it is correct to say that some person is a bachelor where the person is not a male or is married. In order to be a bachelor a person has to be male and he cannot be married. Thus whenever the definiendum correctly applies, so will the definiens. Can we produce an example where the definiens applies but the definiendum does not? A five-second-old baby boy is a male who is not married and yet we would not want to say that he is a bachelor. We have thus produced a counterexample to the definition. Hence the definition is incorrect.

If we had accepted the above definition of being a bachelor, our definition would have been too broad. A reportive definition is too *broad* when the definiens correctly applies to something to which the definiendum does not correctly apply.

We might modify the definition of "bachelor" and say that "bachelor" means *a male of marriageable age who is not married.* This would take care of the above counterexample. Note that being of marriageable age is vague. When exactly is a person of marriageable age? This will vary from culture to culture and even within a culture there will be some indeterminacy. The same comments are true if "bachelor" is defined as *a man who is not married.* When exactly is someone a man as opposed to a mere boy? For legal purposes we can specify an age when a person will be said to be of marriageable age or a man. However this might make our definition too narrow. A reportive definition is too *narrow* when the definiendum correctly applies to something to

---

4. We are not concerned with the sense of "bachelor" in which a young knight was said to be a bachelor, nor the sense in which it is sometimes applied to animals.

which the definiens does not correctly apply. The legal age speci-
fied to be a man might be twenty-one. But as the term "bachelor"
is ordinarily used, we might still wish to call a male who is twenty
a bachelor. Since being of marriageable age is part of the definition
of being a bachelor, and since the expression "being of marriageable age" is vague, the term "bachelor" is also somewhat vague.

Given the modified definition of "bachelor" can we produce a
counterexample to it? We can easily imagine cases where the
definiens would apply and the term "bachelor" would not. If
Jones's wife has recently died, he is a male of marriageable age
who is not married. But he is not a bachelor; he is a widower. Thus
we have produced a counterexample to the modified definition.
To take care of this counterexample, we can again modify the
definition to read:

> "bachelor" means *a male of marriageable age who has
> never been married.*

Can any counterexamples to this definition be produced? Although some interesting examples can be described, we can accept
this modified definition as being basically correct.

To test a reportive definition for correctness, we try to produce
a counterexample to the proposed definition. To construct a
correct reportive definition, we should ask, "What is the established meaning of the expression?" Answering this question is
often very difficult. If the expression has more than one meaning,
we have to isolate the various different senses. We also may find
that competent speakers of the language use the expression in a
slightly different way. For instance some people do not call priests
or the Pope bachelors. By their positions these men are not eligible
for marriage. Others do call priests and the Pope bachelors. For
one group of competent speakers of English, the conditions of
being a bachelor include eligibility whereas for another group
eligibility is not included. Should we say that the word "bachelor"
has a slightly different meaning for each group? Or should we say
that one group is misusing the term? Lack of uniformity of usage
creates a problem when attempting to construct a correct reportive definition.

Vagueness also produces problems. If we are attempting to
construct a correct reportive definition of a term and there are
cases where it is not clear whether the term applies, this can make

it difficult to determine the meaning of the expression. Assume that we are trying to construct a correct reportive definition of the word "war." We can easily imagine cases where it is not clear what we should say. The Cuban missile crisis example is one such case. This makes it difficult to determine what a war is and thus to construct a correct reportive definition.

Dictionary definitions are intended to correctly report established meanings of terms. Frequently such definitions are circular. "Marriage" might be defined as a state of wedlock and "wedlock" in turn might be defined as *being in a state of marriage.* Frequently the meaning of a term to be defined is given by listing a number of expressions that have approximately the same meaning but differ slightly. The dictionary defines "to deceive" as to *mislead, delude, cheat.*[5] Now if a person is deluded he is confused about the truth, but his false belief may not be the result of deception. Thus deception and delusion are not the same. Quite often when one deceives another person he cheats him. But again deception and cheating are not the same. To mislead comes closer to deception than deluding or cheating.

When constructing reportive definitions a dictionary is very helpful, but it does not always provide us with an adequate definition. We may have to modify the definition some. The dictionary defines a war as the state of exerting violence or force against another politically organized body. This definition is not adequate since it does not correctly report the established meaning of the term. As it stands, the definition is too broad since not all instances of exerting violence or force against another political body are wars.

Stipulative definitions do not report the established meaning of a word; instead they assign a meaning to the term. A stipulative definition may be used to introduce an entirely new expression or it may be used to assign a special meaning to a term already in use. We might stipulate that "neutron" is to mean *a particle of charge zero and mass number one.* Here a new term has been introduced and assigned a special meaning. When the word "momentum" is defined as *mass times velocity,* a special meaning is assigned to a term already in use. Stipulative definitions are frequent in technical literature. "Charge," "stimulus," "osmosis," "random sample,"

---

5. All references to the dictionary are to *Webster's New Collegiate Dictionary*, 2d ed. (Springfield, Mass.: G. and C. Merriam, 1960).

and "deep structure" are all technical terms with stipulative definitions. Assigning a special meaning to a term is frequently very useful. The word "force" in its ordinary sense is vague. By stipulating that the term "force" will be used in physics so that force is equal to mass times acceleration, great precision can be introduced.

Since stipulative definitions do not report the ordinary meaning of an expression, they are not open to counterexample. They can, however, be circular. We must be careful not to assign meanings to terms in such a way as to make the resulting stipulative definitions circular.

There is a way of employing stipulative definitions that is fallacious. To the question of whether or not wars are morally wrong, one might reply that wars by definition involve the degradation of humans. Since any act of degrading a human is morally wrong, wars are morally wrong. If the definition of "war" is stipulative and not reportive, the redefinist fallacy has been comitted.[6] The question at issue was whether or not a war as we ordinarily employ the term is morally wrong. A stipulative and not a reportive definition has been given. The term has thus been redefined. On the basis of the special meaning assigned to the term, it has been concluded that the original question has been answered. But the original question has not been answered at all. The question was "In the established sense of 'war,' are wars morally wrong?" The answer that has been given is "In the stipulated sense of 'war,' wars are morally wrong." This is irrelevant to the original question. If the definition were a correct reportive definition, then it would have been shown that wars are wrong. However, since a special sense has been given to the term "war," the original question has not been answered.

Frequently when people argue about the truth or falsity of some statement p, it is claimed "Given the way I use the term W, statement p is true (false)." In such a situation we have to be careful if we are not to commit the redefinist fallacy. Some statement may be true (false) given the way a particular individual employs a certain term. It does not follow from this that the statement is true (false) given the *customary* sense of the term.

---

6. The name "redefinist fallacy" comes from James W. Cornman and Keith Lehrer, *Philosophical Problems and Arguments: An Introduction* (New York: Macmillan, 1968), pp. 23-24.

A third type of explicit definition is the *reconstructive definition.* Such a definition is based on the established meaning of the term being defined and yet it also involves a stipulative aspect. If an expression *W* is somewhat vague as it is ordinarily used, it may be very useful for certain purposes to define the term in such a way as to make it more precise. The definition would not simply be a report of the ordinary meaning of the term, nor would it simply be a stipulation that the term was to be used in a certain way. It would involve a synthesis of the two. A reconstructive definition reconstructs the ordinary sense of the expression in order to make it more precise.

Consider the way we ordinarily employ the word "know" in such sentences as "Jones knows that it is raining." The dictionary states that in this sense of "know" the above sentence means that on the basis of information that Jones has, he recognizes it as a fact that it is raining. This is vague. In this sense of "know" do we ever know that scientific laws are true? Since "know" as it is ordinarily used is somewhat vague, it would be useful in discussing the above question to make the meaning of the term more precise. To do this we can give a reconstructive definition. The sense of "know" that we are interested in might be reconstructed as meaning *to have a justified true belief.* We know a scientific law is true if we believe the law is true, it is in fact true, and we can justify our belief by appealing to the evidence. The reconstructive definition that is given is based on the customary sense of the expression only the new definition makes it more precise.

Since a reconstructive definition is intended to make the customary sense of a term more precise, it must conform to the basic meaning of the term. One way to criticize a reconstructive definition is to argue that it omits an essential part of the meaning of the term or it adds an important element that is foreign to the term's ordinary meaning. In either case the definition would fail to conform to the basic meaning of the term. Important terms such as "truth," "cause," "probable," "civil disobedience," "violence," "revolution" are somewhat vague. Reconstructive definitions are useful when discussing questions involving these terms.[7]

7. For a good discussion of definitions see Carl G. Hempel, *Fundamentals of Concept Formation in Empirical Science* (Chicago: University of Chicago Press, 1952), chap. i. See also James D. Carney and Richard K. Scheer, *Fundamentals of Logic* (New York: Macmillan, 1964), chap. iii, and Irving M. Copi, *Introduction to Logic,* 4th ed. (New York: Macmillan, 1972), chap. iv.

Exercises

A. Do the following sentences involve any confusion?

  1. Mark Twain was the pseudonym of Samuel Clemens.

  2. War is violent is grammatical.

B. Are the following correct reportive definitions? Use the method of counterexample to test the definitions.

  1. "Civil disobedience" means *any protest against the government.*

  2. "Democratic form of government" means *a form of government where the political power is retained by the people and is exercised either directly or indirectly through a system of representation.*

  3. "To be just" means *to treat people consistently.*

  4. "Violence" means *any action that damages a person or object.*

  5. "Patriotism" means *devotion to the welfare of one's country.*

  6. "To lie" means *to utter a falsehood with the intent to deceive.*

Answers to Selected Exercises

A.

  1. The *man* Mark Twain was not the pseudonym; the *name* was. Hence the sentence should read: "Mark Twain" was the pseudonym of Samuel Clemens.

B.

  1. If Russia lodges a protest against our government, it does not follow that it is an act of civil disobedience. Since there are counterexamples, the definition is not a correct reportive definition.

  3. If you treat people consistently in an unjust way, you are unjust. Thus there are counterexamples to the definition.

5. This is an acceptable definition.

4-3 Entailment and Consistency

Entailment and consistency are two very important logical notions that deserve special mention. Statements bear various logical relations to other statements. One of these logical relations is that of entailment. We are frequently interested in what a statement entails. For instance what does the statement that Jones committed an act of civil disobedience entail? A statement p is said to *entail* a statement q just in case it is impossible for p to be true and q to be false. Thus if p entails q and p is true, it follows that q must be true. The statement "Jones is a bachelor" entails the statement "Jones is a man." Part of the definition of being a bachelor is that the person is a man. Thus it is not possible for the first statement to be true and the second one false. The first statement also entails the statement that Jones has never been married. Never having been married is again part of the definition of being a bachelor.

To test whether a statement p entails a statement q, we try to describe a possible example where p would be true and yet where q would be false. Again the example does not have to be something that has actually happened or ever will happen, but it does have to be something that could possibly occur. If we can produce such an example, then p does not entail q. If we cannot produce such an example, we may *tentatively* accept the entailment relation. The method of testing entailment relations also will be called the *method of counterexample.* To take an example, suppose someone claimed that "Jones is an unmarried male" entails "Jones is a bachelor." To show that this entailment relation does not hold, we produce a counterexample. As previously noted, a five-second-old baby boy is a male who is not married and yet he is not a bachelor. Thus we can imagine a possible situation where the statement "Jones is an unmarried male" is true and yet the statement "Jones is a bachelor" is false. Hence the first statement does not entail the second one.

Notice, however, that no counterexample can be produced where the statement "Jones is a bachelor" would be true and the statement "Jones is an unmarried male" would be false. Part of the definition of being a bachelor is being an unmarried male, hence being a bachelor entails being an unmarried male. Appealing to definitions or meaning is important when trying to show that one statement entails another.

One way to show that a statement p is false is to show that p entails a false statement q. If p entails q and q is false, then p also must be false. For example, suppose Smith claims that Jones's protest was an act of civil disobedience, and imagine that his protest did not involve a violation of any law. If a protest is an act of civil disobedience, this entails that the act violated a law. Since Jones's protest did not involve a violation of any law, Smith's claim has been shown to be false.

Consistency is another important logical notion. A statement p is said to be *inconsistent* if it cannot possibly be true. Consider the statement "God exists and God does not exist." This statement is inconsistent since it cannot both be the case that God exists and God does not exist. Statements having the form "*p* and not-*p*" are *explicit contradictions.* Such statements cannot possibly be true. Hence all explicit contradictions are inconsistent. But some inconsistent statements are not explicit contradictions. For example the statement "A bachelor is a female" is inconsistent but it is not an explicit contradiction. Although it is not an explicit contradiction, it entails such a statement. To show that a statement is inconsistent we must show that it is an explicit contradiction or else that it entails an explicit contradiction. By definition to be a bachelor is to be a male, and by definition to be a female is not to be a male. Hence the statement "A bachelor is a female" entails the explicit contradiction that a bachelor is a male and a bachelor is not a male.

Notice the difference between a statement that is false and hence is not true and a statement that could not possibly be true. The statement "The Empire State Building is at present the tallest building in the United States" is false. However it is not inconsistent. We can easily imagine a possible situation where the statement would be true. For example suppose that all the buildings as tall or taller than the Empire State Building fell down. If this situation occurred, then the statement "The Empire State Building is at present the tallest building in the United States" would be true. An inconsistent statement is one that could never under any circumstances be true. It is false and would be false in any possible situation. Examples of false statements that are not inconsistent are:

(1)   Wars never involve killings.

(2) The average life span of a human being is 100.
(3) There is no pollution problem in the world.
(4) All men love one another.

Here are some examples of inconsistent statements:

(5) Wars do not involve hostility, force, or violence.
(6) It is your moral duty to keep a promise and it is morally permissible for you not to.
(7) 2 is greater than 4 and 2 is not greater than 4.
(8) All men love one another but some men do not.

Although all the statements in the first set are false, we can imagine circumstances where they would be true. We cannot do this for the statements in the second set. Consider (1) and (5). Part of the definition of a war is that it involves great hostility, force, or violence. Since this is part of the definition of a war, we cannot imagine a situation where (5) would be true. (5) thus entails the explicit contradiction that a war involves hostility, force, or violence and a war does not involve hostility, force, or violence. Although (1) is false, since wars usually do involve killing, we can imagine wars that involve great hostility, force, or violence where, fortunately, no one is killed. (1) does not entail an explicit contradiction. Thus (1) is false but is not inconsistent whereas (5) is inconsistent. Again we can imagine a situation where (4) would be true. But (8) entails the explicit contradiction that all men love one another and not all men love one another.

The reason the notion of an inconsistent statement is important is that such a statement cannot be true. Thus one way to show that a statement is false is to show that it is inconsistent. To show that it is inconsistent, we show that it is an explicit contradiction or else that it entails such a statement. Statement (6) above is inconsistent since part of what is meant by saying that something is your moral duty is that it is not morally permissible for you not to do that thing. (6) thus entails the explicit contradiction that it is morally permissible for you not to keep a promise and it is not morally permissible for you not to keep a promise.

A *set* of statements $p_1, p_2, \ldots, p_n$ is inconsistent if it is not possible for all the members of the set to be true. Consider the following set of statements:

(1) To conscientiously object to a war one must object to all wars.

(2) Jones conscientiously objects to the war in Indochina since he feels it is an immoral war.

(3) Jones would not object to a war fought in self-defense.

The set of statements is inconsistent. If conscientiously objecting to a war entails objecting to all wars, then Jones cannot conscientiously object to the war in Indochina if he does not object to all wars. It follows that at least one member of the set of statements is false. The importance of the notion of an inconsistent set of statements is that if we can show that a set of statements is inconsistent, it follows that at least one of the statements is false.

Exercises

A. Do the following entailment relations hold?

1. "Jones is unable to read or write" entails "Jones is illiterate."

2. "There is a revolution" entails "There is great violence."

3. "Jones has the true belief that it is raining" entails "Jones knows that it is raining."

4. "Jones know that it is raining" entails "It is raining."

5. "If all men are equal, then they should be treated equally" entails "If not all men are equal, then they should not be treated equally."

6. "10 is an even number" entails "10 is divisible by 2."

B. Which of the following statements are inconsistent?

1. Jones is human and he has no heart.

2. Jones is married and yet he has no wife.

3. Jones's two wives both claim correctly that he is a monogamist.

4. This monkey is not a primate.

5. Sally threw a brick out the window and it did not fall.

6. Jones loves everyone but he does not love himself.

C. Which of the following sets of statements are inconsistent?

1. Jones is patriotic. He went to Washington and protested the war. The protest was not in the best interests of the nation.

2. A statement is true or false. If a statement is true or false, then it is meaningful. The statement "My dream was three times the size of yours" makes no sense.

3. Since God created the world, this must be the best of all possible worlds. It is the best of all possible worlds only if there is no unnecessary evil. The death and destruction of children in war is an unnecessary evil.

Answers to Selected Exercises

A.

1. If Jones's being unable to read or write is due to his not having learned how to do these things, then it follows he is illiterate. But if Jones's being unable to read or write is due to something such as an accident, it does not follow he is illiterate.

3. No, since his belief may not be based on any evidence. Even though his belief is true, it does not follow he knows that it is raining.

5. No, for if we assume that the first statement is true, it does not follow that if all men are not equal, they should not be treated equally. Perhaps they should be treated equally. A statement of the form "If p, then q" does not entail a statement of the form "If not-p, then not-q."

B.

1. This could be true so it is not inconsistent. Perhaps he has had his heart removed and has some special gadget.

3. This is inconsistent. If his wives' claims are correct, he cannot be a monogamist.

5. This is not inconsistent. There may be some reason why the brick did not fall.

C.

1. The set is not inconsistent. If Jones is patriotic, he loves his country and is greatly concerned about its welfare. Perhaps that is why he protested. Even if the protest was not in the best interests of the nation, it does not follow he is not patriotic.

3. The set is inconsistent. It is claimed that this is the best of all possible worlds and that if it is the best of all possible worlds, then there is no unnecessary evil. Finally it is claimed that there is unnecessary evil. These statements entail the explicit contradiction that it is the best of all possible worlds and it is not the best of all possible worlds.

4-4 Summary of Basic Concepts

1. A word W or a sentence S is ambiguous if it has more than one meaning and from the context it cannot be determined which meaning is intended.

2. An expression W is *vague* if there are cases where it cannot be determined whether W applies, and this indeterminacy of application is due to the meaning of W, not to a lack of evidence.

3. A *reportive definition* reports the established meaning of the expression; a *stipulative definition* stipulates what meaning an expression is to have; a *reconstructive definition* reconstructs the established meaning of an expression to make it more precise.

4. A statement p *entails* a statement q just in case it is impossible for p to be true and q to be false.

5. A statement p is *inconsistent* if it cannot possibly be true; an *explicit contradiction* is a statement of the form "p and not-p." To show that a statement is inconsistent show that it is an explicit contradiction or that it entails an explicit contradiction. A set of statements is inconsistent if not all the members of the set can be true.

Exercises

Carefully explain your answers and give examples wherever appropriate.

1. Can we understand the meaning of an expression if it is vague?

2. Explain the difference between ambiguity and vagueness.

3. How can the correctness of a reportive definition be tested?

4. Does this method apply to stipulative and reconstructive definitions?

5. What is a circular definition?

6. What is the redefinist fallacy?

7. How do we test to see if a statement p entails a statement q?

8. What is the importance of consistency?

9. If a statement is an explicit contradiction, does it follow that it is inconsistent?

10. If a statement is inconsistent, does it follow that it is an explicit contradiction?

11. If p entails q, is the set of the statements consisting of p and not-q consistent?

12. If p entails an inconsistent statement, does it follow that p is false?

5

Argumentative Essays

5-1 Constructing and Evaluating Argumentative Essays

So far we have considered how to construct and critically evaluate arguments. These same techniques can be applied to constructing and evaluating argumentative essays. In an argumentative essay a thesis is stated and supported by arguments. Quite often a number of major theses are advanced.

The suggestions which follow should prove to be helpful when reading and evaluating an argumentative essay. First, such an essay must be read carefully. It is not like reading a novel. Frequently the reader must recognize subtle distinctions and grasp complex arguments. An argumentative essay must be read with the same care with which one would read an essay in physics.

It is helpful to begin by glancing over the essay to see how it is organized. Usually this makes it easier to identify the main theses and the supporting arguments. Next, read the entire essay to see what the author's main points are and how the whole essay is organized. The essay should now be reread more carefully paying greater attention to details. Isolate the arguments in support of the main theses. Having identified the main points and isolated the arguments in support of them, you can begin to critically evaluate the essay.

When critically evaluating an argumentative essay, there are a number of questions to ask. Have the main theses been formulated clearly? If they have been expressed in a vague or ambiguous way, they may need to be rephrased. The meaning of important terms may be left unspecified and definitions may be required.

If the main theses are formulated clearly, the next question to ask is whether the arguments in support of them are logically correct. This requires you to identify the author's arguments and to put them into standard form, a task which is frequently difficult. Once the arguments have been identified and put into standard form, you should determine if they are deductively valid, inductively strong, or neither.

If the arguments are logically correct, you then should attempt to determine whether the premises are true. If they are true, the conclusions have been shown to be true or at least probably true. To be in a position to evaluate the truth of the premises requires one to understand the meaning of them. Some of the premises may be used ambiguously or an expression contained in one of them may be so vague that one cannot assess the truth of the premises. If the author has attempted to specify the meaning of various terms by giving definitions, you should determine what type of definition is given. If a definition is intended to be reportive, does it correctly report the ordinary meaning of the expression or can a counterexample to the definition be produced? If a definition is stipulative, has the redefinist fallacy been committed? If a reconstructive definition is given, does it make the customary sense more precise? Once the meaning of the premises is clear and they are sufficiently precise, you can begin to evaluate their truth or falsity. Do the premises entail any false statements? Are the premises consistent? Can you give an argument to show that at least one of the premises is false?

When writing argumentative essays, the same general questions should be kept in mind. What are the main points that you are trying to make? Frequently the main point of an essay is not stated in a precise enough way. Definitions are required sometimes to remedy this problem. If the main theses are expressed clearly, what are your arguments in support of them? These arguments should be expressed in standard form and they must be logically correct. Oftentimes we do not adequately support our assertions; we argue about irrelevant issues, talk in generalities without sufficient evidence, or base an argument on only part of the evidence. If the arguments are logically correct, the next question to be asked is whether the premises are all true. Are they expressed clearly and can you adequately support them?

5-2 An Example

The following selection is an argumentative essay by Rudolph H. Weingartner entitled "Justifying Civil Disobedience." The essay should be read *very carefully* and critically evaluated. The questions at the end of the selection should help you to evaluate the essay.

JUSTIFYING CIVIL DISOBEDIENCE

Rudolph H. Weingartner[1]

I

In general, we ought to obey the law. Suppose I ask whether   1
I should do A or B; if you then tell me that to do A is to
break the law, surely this information must weigh on the
side of B and count against A. It is not a conclusive reason
for not doing A, for, as I shall suggest, the arguments designed to show that breaking the law is never justified are
not successful. What the truth of this generalization does
show, however, is that any breach of the law is in *need* of a
justification, that it is not one of those matters—like telling
the truth or being kind to children—that requires justification only under special circumstances.

   This may be obvious in most cases of lawbreaking, but it   2
seems not to be so obvious when it comes to civil disobedi-

Reprinted from *The Columbia Forum,* Spring 1966, Vol. IX, No. 2. Copyright 1966 by The Trustees of Columbia University in the City of New York. Revised in 1968. Reprinted with permission of *The Columbia Forum* and the author.
   1. I have learned much from the following: Hugo A. Bedau, "On Civil Disobe-
dience," *Journal of Philosophy,* 58 (1969); Charles L. Black, Jr., "The Problem of the
Compatibility of Civil Disobedience with American Institutions of Government," *Texas
Law Review,* 43 (1965); Carl Cohen, "Essence and Ethics of Civil Disobedience," *The
Nation,* 198 (1964); John Dickinson, "A Working Theory of Sovereignity II," *Political
Science Quarterly,* 43 (1928); Morris Keeton, "The Morality of Civil Disobedience,"
Texas Law Review, 43 (1965); Harold Laski, *The State in Theory and Practice,* New
York, 1935; Richard A. Wasserstrom, "The Obligation to Obey the Law," *UCLA Law
Review,* 10 (1963).

ence. Indeed, so much passion has of late been aroused by
the issue of civil disobedience that we are scarcely aware of
the lack of clarity in our thinking about the subject. More
than one commentator discussing the rioting and violence in
the Watts district of Los Angeles in the summer of 1965
used the term "civil disobedience" in referring to events and
actions to which it certainly does not apply. Before discussing its justification it would be well to consider what civil
disobedience is.

Civil disobedience is, above all, disobedience. It is the vio-   3
lation of a command issued by an authority, such as a government, that has a claim to our obedience. When a number of
people disobey a bank official who asks them to leave the
bank to cease immobilizing it by perpetually requesting
coins to be changed into bills and bills into coins, it is not
civil disobedience, unless a law is also broken. The law has a
claim to our obedience; bank officials as such do not. Where
a government is not directly confronted in an illegal act,
there may be a strike, a boycott, harassment, or some other
kind of pressure, but not civil disobedience. Nor is *legal*
non-obedience of the law civil disobedience. Conscientious
objectors are exempted from service in the armed forces,
and Jehovah's Witnesses are permitted to refrain from salut-
ing the flag. Neither group is engaged in civil disobedience.

Moreover, civil disobedience must be *civil* disobedience of   4
a law. If those who disobey the law use violence in doing so,
they are no longer practicing civil disobedience. For while
the violence may overtly be aimed at private persons, it is at
least implicitly directed against those charged with enforcing the law. But to that extent the act is no longer confined
to the transgression of a particular law; instead it becomes a
defiance of the authority that makes and enforces the laws.
Violent disobedience is not simply a noisier kind of civil
disobedience; it is rebellion.

This distinction is an important one. Rebellion or revolu-   5
tion, whether it is peaceful or violent, aims to modify the
established order either by supplanting those who make and
enforce the law, or by changing the very processes of legislation and enforcement, or by doing both. The change sought
is not simply a change in one or another law, but of the entire framework within which laws are made and carried out.

Accordingly, insofar as Gandhi aimed at the elimination of British rule in India, he was a revolutionary, for civil disobedience aims at a particular law or governmental measure, and not at the state itself. An important though not infallible symbol of this distinction is that in the clearest cases of civil disobedience those engaged in it are willing to accept the punishment that is meted out to those who break the law in question. They use violence neither in disobeying the law nor in their reaction to arrest, trial, and the sentencing that may follow disobedience.

But surely, most people who disobey a law non-violently are not thereby practicing civil disobedience. A person may knowingly park in a no-parking zone hoping not to get caught and be ready, if not happy, to pay the fine if he is so unlucky as to be found out. Still, this does not make him a practitioner of civil disobedience. Whoever engages in civil disobedience commits an illegal act because he takes a law or governmental measure to be wrong; he seeks to protest and possibly to change a wrong done by the state, pitting what he takes to be right—that is to say moral—against what the state takes to be right--that is to say, at least legal. There is no type of law or governmental measure which is, by its nature, immune to civil disobedience; moreover, the *way* in which a law or measure might be found wanting must be left open. Some laws are protested because they are thought unjust; others because they are taken to transgress a divine commandment; some because they are thought to violate rights possessed by all men; still others because they are held to produce effects contrary to the common good. To say that the goal must be moral requires that the illegal act not be undertaken simply to gain an advantage for the actor. And because it is not always so clear what someone's purposes may be (including one's own), the willingness to accept punishment is a useful sign that the disobedience is not simply the means to a private end.   6

It does not follow from this that a Negro can never employ genuine civil disobedience in order to bring about civil rights for Negroes, or that his actions must be seen as self-seeking, however understandable—analogous, say, to a steelworker's strike for higher wages. A Negro practitioner of civil disobedience will undoubtedly be better off if he suc-   7 ceeds in bringing about a change in the laws. But the question of purposes is not settled by such a consideration of effects. If an illegal act is performed in order to protest against a law for being unjust or contrary to the good of the community, then it is civil disobedience, even if justice or the common good is also to the advantage of the protester. What remains of fundamental importance for the identification of an act of civil disobedience and for its justification alike is that the purposes of the act be moral.

Finally, the activity of civil disobedience must be public.   8
Simple evasion of the law, even when undertaken for the highest reasons of conscience, is not yet civil disobedience. The physician, for example, who quietly administers a fatal injection to an incurable patient in order to relieve great suffering evades a law but does not engage in civil disobedience. Even if the doctor is resigned to accepting punishment should he be found out, his act is not civil disobedience unless he intends his transgression to be publicly known. Civil disobedience *usually* involves an unwillingness to obey a law thought to be wrong, but it always constitutes a protest against a law or governmental measure. And a protest is more than the expression of a disagreement; it includes a desire for a change. As such, the evasion of a law makes no contribution to getting a law or policy revoked or modified. For an act of conscience to be also one of protest, it must at least potentially be able to persuade others. That the whole town knew of Thoreau's imprisonment was not adventitious: it was a part of his civil disobedience.

An act of civil disobedience, to sum up, is an illegal, non-   9
violent, moral, and public protest against a law or governmental measure.

I want also to distinguish between two types of civil dis-   10
obedience, *direct* and *indirect,* a difference that will have a bearing on the question of justification. In some cases of civil disobedience, the very law that is being protested against is the one disobeyed. It is direct civil disobedience when a law calls for the separate seating of whites and Negroes, and a person violates that very law because he thinks it is wrong. But in many instances, civil disobedience cannot take so straightforward a form. The suffragettes who fought for women's rights could not disobey the law that disenfran-

chised them. These militant ladies violated trespassing laws, statutes against disturbing the peace, and the like.

Clearly, indirect civil disobedience is the only kind that is possible when the wrong being protested is the *absence* of a law or a governmental measure. But often, too, indirect civil disobedience is the only possible form of disobedience when the protest is directed against a law or measure that *does* exist. The ordinary citizen, for example, cannot readily interfere with the testing of nuclear arms or the appropriation of money for the war, so that the law or command to be disobeyed will have to be different from that being protested against. The connection between the object of protest and the measure violated may be close: the suffragettes disturbed the peace at political meetings of campaigners who did not support the proposal to give women the vote. At other times there is no intrinsic connection at all: Bertrand Russell was arrested for refusing to keep the peace as a protest against nuclear arms.

11

II

Society requires order for its existence. Throughout history this need has been affirmed with passion and pursued with singlemindedness. It is thus not surprising that many men have held that one is never justified in breaking a law and that civil disobedience is always wrong. On the other hand, in more than one reformation has the conscience of the individual been raised above the rules of institutions and the mores of society. Accordingly, we have been urged never to obey a law that we think is wrong. In this view civil disobedience is then always justified when directed against laws that conflict with one's convictions. I think both of these views are wrong and I shall furthermore argue that there cannot even be a general rule which serves to decide when civil disobedience is justified and when it is not.

1

Some have claimed that it is never morally right to disobey the law because morality simply consists in obedience to the laws. This is an ancient doctrine that tries to define what is right wholly in terms of what the laws say is right. And its reputation is equally old. Laws conflict at least from one period to another and from place to place; if rightness

2

were constituted by what the laws dictate, then we are led
to the weird conclusion that the same act can be both right
and not right, or, whenever the law is silent, be neither right
nor not right. Moreover, this logical identification of morality with law would make it meaningless nonsense to evaluate
a law: to censure a law as unjust or to praise it as in accord
with morality would have to be considered as unintelligible
as criticizing squares for having right angles or praising them
for having sides that are straight.

Then, it has been held that any law which fails to conform   3
to the demands of morality is not truly a law. But surely
this is an odd view of the nature of laws. It makes well-nigh
irrelevant to their character as laws their creation and prom-
ulgation by a properly constituted legislature, their enforcement by a legitimate executive, and their application by an
acknowledged judiciary. To define the legal in terms of the
moral makes little more sense than to define the moral in
terms of the legal.

Others have granted that morality and legality can and do   4
diverge, but they nevertheless hold that one is never justified in disobeying a law, because of the difficulties of *determining* what is right. Their argument may be formulated in
this way:

Societies differ greatly in the ways in which their laws are   5
made. The law of the land may be the word of a single, un-
questioned sovereign, or the produce of assemblies in which
all the people participate. Secular authorites create and interpret the laws in some societies; in others, a special priest-
ly class reads the will of the gods. But no group of men that
is rightly called a society is without a relatively stable method for answering the question, what does the law say with
regard to this matter? It may be a difficult one to answer,
but at least it is always possible to point to some social institutions whose job it is to answer it, and to standards, however crude, by which the adequacy of any answer can be
answered.

The moral realm is not similarly favored. Individuals and   6
groups, some more powerful than others, all have opinions
as to what is right. While there may be much agreement,
there is also conflict. Above all, there is no recognized authority to adjudicate moral disputes. No doubt, it is then

argued, there are differences between what is right and what legal, but there is no institution that determines whether what someone thinks to be wrong actually *is* wrong. Accordingly, no one is ever justified in disobeying a law on the grounds that the law is wrong, for who can say what is right?

Two replies can be made to this objection to civil disobedience. First, the lack of an institution for making moral decisions does not imply that there cannot be reasons—even conclusive reasons—in support of a moral claim. Whatever may be the conditions for definitiveness in moral judgment, the existence of special institutions is surely not a necessary one, however much their existence may help in securing agreement. And agreement is precisely what should not be expected. More often than not, the moral critic of the law proposes to apply to the law a higher, a finer, or a more advanced standard of morality than do the institutions that make and interpret the laws. In a democracy at least, these legal institutions can be expected to be quite close to the moral norm of the community, so that the critic is not likely to find pervasive assent to his views.

Second, the lack of an institution for determining what is right is not sufficient ground for failing to do what one thinks is right. For there is never an institution that dispenses the correct answer and secures everyone's agreement to boot. While not everything we do is as grave as civil disobedience, some acts we perform, such as begetting children or going off to war—acts that do not conflict with the laws—are at least of equal gravity. Yet neither the lack of a sure method of decision nor the absence of agreement should or does stop us from acting. What one thinks is right does not always turn out to be so, but it would be strange advice never to do what one thinks is right simply because others do not agree or because one *might* be wrong.

This leads to a final group of arguments in support of the thesis that civil disobedience is never justified. These arguments claim, in various ways, that the social consequences of civil disobedience are always worse than those of obedience. "What if everyone did it?" is the question to which a fatal sting is attributed; and of course the prospect of a society in which no one obeys the law is frightening. But just

7

8

9

what is the connection between one person's act of civil disobedience and the chaos of a lawless society? Surely it is
evident that such an act does not actually bring about the
commission of countless other breaches of law. Indeed, an
act of civil disobedience may confirm more citizens in their
legal rectitude than it induces to break laws. What causes
what is a question of empirical fact, and observation simply
fails to bear out the contention that *everyone* will do what
somebody does. And if it is argued that the risk of violence,
the suffering of punishment, and other such consequences
of disobeying the law will always be worse than those of
obedience to the law, I must reply that this is all too gran-
diose a claim about the way of the world. Whether the consequences of one act are better or worse than those of
another is a matter of looking and seeing; to say that one
type of act *must* be better than another, regardless of the
circumstances, is not warranted by any general law about
human behavior.

What now of the other side of the controversy? Have not   10
the floodgates been opened to the view that whenever one
thinks the law to be wrong, civil disobedience is justified?
Laws ought to be obeyed, some have maintained, only when
and if they are morally right. And who else but each person
himself can judge the moral adequacy of the law? When he
judges the law to be morally deficient, he is at least *justified*
in disobeying it and possibly *obligated* to do so. It is even
held that men who do not act on what they think is right
give up their function as citizens; surely, it is argued, men
give up their dignity as moral agents unless they themselves
determine what they ought to do.

There is a nobility to this position which makes it an at-   11
tractive one; nevertheless I think that it is at best confused.
First there is the matter of conscientiousness: I might take a
law to be wrong on the basis of quick and superficial
thought or I might come to this conclusion after prolonged
reflection. I may be ignorant of the issues involved or I may
have made a special study of them. The following sentence,
accordingly, is not paradoxical, but merely expresses the
complexity of moral judgments: "I think this law is morally
wrong, but because you are more knowledgeable than I
about its long-range effects, I concede that you may be right

in saying that the law is good." If civil disobedience is justified when one thinks a law to be wrong, then surely it is justified only to the degree to which one is entitled to one's opinion.

Second, there is a vast difference between judging that a law is wrong and judging that one ought to disobey it. Even if I am correct in thinking that a particular law requires an act that is morally wrong (or the omission of one that is needed), it by no means just follows that I should disobey it. For many other considerations must enter into a decision to disobey a law, even after the question of the rightness of the law has been already settled. It is not self-contradictory to say that such and such a law is wrong, but that it ought to be obeyed. One is therefore not automatically justified in disobeying *any* law one thinks is wrong, much less in protesting publicly against it. 12

It has now been shown, I think, that the extreme positions on the justifiability of civil disobedience are difficult to maintain: civil disobedience is neither prohibited nor permitted by some perfectly general formula. Indeed, there is no simple way of dealing with the ethics of civil disobedience, for it can be demonstrated that there cannot even be a rule that serves to decide when civil disobedience is and when it is not justified. 13

Surely, one might contend, all those cases in which civil disobedience is justified share some characteristic, simple or complex, that the unjustifiable ones do not possess. And in a sense, this is indeed true. One may be justified in disobeying a law if, after one has conscientiously reflected on all the relevant factors, one has good evidence that a greater good is achieved by breaking than by obeying it. Correct or not, this rule is at least plausible; still it will not serve to decide when one is justified in breaking a law. How much reflection is conscientious reflection? Which factors are relevant factors? How much evidence is good evidence? And which goods are greater than which? These questions are not simple ones and for none is the answer the same for all possible cases. (What is good enough evidence for breaking a date need not be good enough for breaking the engagement.) 14

We should agree to accept such a rule and cease asking 15

which cases of civil disobedience are justified. But in ex-
change we inherit the new problem of finding out to which
cases the rule applies. The gain is only apparent: the sim-
plicity of a wholesale solution is illusory.

III

We are now left with the requirement that each case of civil   1
disobedience must be examined on its own merits. The best
that we can do is to spell out what some of the relevant considerations are which help to decide whether or not a case
of civil disobedience is justified. It will be convenient to discuss these issues under five general headings, though I have
no illusions that the list is exhaustive.

1. *The wrongness of the law.* Civil disobedience is justi-   2
fied to the degree to which the object of the protest is
thought to be wrong. If the law or measure is not thought
to be wrong at all, breaking it does not constitute civil disobedience; if it is thought to be wrong only in a trivial or
minor way, its wrongness cannot outweigh either the general obligation we have to obey the law or the disadvan-
tageous consequences of civil disobedience. If the wrong is
thought to be grievous, civil disobedience may be more
readily justified.

Two comments. It is assumed here, as it is throughout this   3
essay, that, in principle, questions of right and wrong have
answers, even if in fact we often fail to arrive at them. Such
a view of morals as objective, however, does not require us
to suppose that there are simple moral absolutes holding for
all times and places. Rather, to hold that criteria in ethics
are objective and to say that moral questions have answers is
to assert above all that what is right or wrong is conceptual-
ly independent of what happens to be thought right or
wrong—by a few people or even by all. (Just as the shape of
the earth is independent of what it is thought to be at any
time or place.) Accordingly, it cannot be enough that the
law is *thought* to be wrong: the question as to whether it *is*
wrong is relevant too.

Second, whether the case of civil disobedience is direct or   4
indirect is relevant here. One's protest is, I think, more
readily justified when it involves the breaking of a law that

is thought to be wrong, rather than some other law. The reason is not complicated. In the case of indirect civil disobedience, the wrongness of the law serves as a reason for the *protest* against it. But in those cases of civil disobedience in which the law that is not obeyed is the same law against which the protest is made, the law's wrongness has an additional function as well. On the general grounds that one ought to do what is right and refrain from doing what is wrong, the wrongness of a law helps to justify *any* willing failure to obey it and since civil disobedience is not only protest but also disobedience, the wrongness of the law plays a dual role in the justification of direct civil disobedience.

2. *The purity and strength of the motive.* It is perfectly   5
possible to believe a law to be wrong but to act against it for self-seeking reasons. "Of course it is a bad law," someone might think, "but I will protest against it because it reduces my income." If one is to be genuinely engaged in civil disobedience, the act of protest must be performed *because* a law is thought to be wrong; the motive must be moral. Yet, it may very well be true that there is no such thing as an unmixed motive; thus, if there is to be justified civil disobedience, it must at least be *relatively* free of an admixture of self-seeking motives. Not only the desire for personal gain counts against the justifiability of an act of civil disobedience; there are other, more subtle, temptations: the desire for fame or revenge, or for the grateful thanks from the underdog, or the anticipation of that special pleasure that may come from breaking the law. The purer and stronger the motive for setting right a wrong, the more readily a person is justified in performing an act of civil disobedience.

But not always when we ask whether an instance of civil   6
disobedience is justified are we interested in whether some— or any—particular *person* was justified in doing what he did. Frequently, our concern in justifying civil disobedience is with the act as abstracted from the individuals who perform it. Motives, thus, have no place in the discussion; we ask only the other questions relevant to the justification of civil disobedience. But to ignore motives in this way is not tantamount to remaining neutral with regard to them. We are not asking whether an act of civil disobedience is justified on

the supposition that the motive of the person who performs it either is or is not moral; on the contrary, as we reflect about the justifiability of an act of civil disobedience, we assume that it is done for moral reasons, that the person was not simply hired, for example. This is what we take as given as we go on to inquire whether the act can be justified with respect to the other considerations relevant to justifying civil disobedience.

3. *The foreseeable consequences of the act.* One's esti- mate of what the consequences of engaging in civil disobedi- ence are likely to be in a particular case is relevant to the justification of that case. To begin with, it makes a differ- ence whether or not there is a likelihood of the act's being successful in bringing about the desired change. But there is no simple relation between probability of success and justi- fication. If one's aim in the commission of an act of civil disobedience is fundamentally utilitarian, it will be harder to justify it, if the chances of success in bringing about the desired change are poor or absent than when they are excel- lent. Perhaps rebellion is called for, perhaps acquiescence. Still, if success in changing the law is more or less ruled out, there remains both the possibility of the creation of a moral climate *favorable* to future success, as well as the danger of public reaction *against* the very cause of the persons in- volved. And, depending upon the degree to which the law is thought to be wrong, one is justified in acting with greater or lesser expectations of success. On the other hand, if the person who engages in civil disobedience does so simply in order to manifest his belief that the law is wrong (however much he may *also* desire that the law be changed), the likeli- hood of the law's actually being changed is not a relevant consideration to the justifying of civil disobedience. In short, the relevance of success to the justification of an act of civil disobedience depends in part upon the *kind* of moral motive that plays a role in the performance of an act of civil disobedience.

Other consequences one must consider are what the risks may be that individuals and groups will in one or another way be harmed. It is more difficult to justify civil disobedi- ence when the danger of violence is great, when not only those actually disobeying the law, but also officers of the

7

8

government and innocent bystanders are likely to be hurt. Furthermore, the consequences for those who propose to engage in civil disobedience must be taken into consideration. If the punishment for breaking the law can be expected to be extremely severe, the commission of civil disobedience (always assuming other things to be equal) is less justified, for we do have duties to ourselves as well as to others. And from the consideration of these consequences for bystanders and actors follows a corollary that seems paradoxical. Still, it is true that where the agents of the state—the police and the judiciary—are cruel and punitive in the extreme, civil disobedience is not likely to be justified. In Nazi Germany of 1940, say, civil disobedience would have been pathetically inappropriate: a certain minimum level of civilization must be attained before civil disobedience can be justified; below it only evasion or rebellion—or acquiescence—are justifiable.

Finally, the more likely it is that the protest involved in   9
civil disobedience can be confined to the law or measure thought to be wrong, the more readily can civil disobedience be justified. If there is in fact a clear danger that committing civil disobedience will spread to other laws, to lawlessness generally, or to a defiance of the state itself, then (again other things being equal) the justification of civil disobedience will be more difficult. For then what must be justifiable is not the single act of civil disobedience, but the lawlessness or revolution which is the likely consequence of that act. But the justification of this is a separate issue.

4. *The availability of alternative methods of reform.* It   10
matters whether other techniques for modifying or revoking the law are available—for example, a cogent presentation at a public hearing. Civil disobedience is much more likely to be justified if the chances of change through legal means are remote.

Only an outline of what is involved in this question of al-   11
ternative methods of reform can be included here. There are two broad classes of alternatives, the legal and the political; and in a society such as ours each has several modes. Both the federalist system and the system of common law provide more than one type of legal recourse in the case of a law thought to be wrong. And politically, the separation of

the legislative and the executive functions alone means that
there is more than one avenue of approach to the government, not to mention the many different techniques by
means of which it can be subjected to pressure. Civil disobedience is more readily justified, the fewer alternative methods there are and the less likely it is that alternative methods will be successful.

It has been maintained that in a democracy, because there   12
is always an alternative method and because success by legal
or political methods is at least in principle always possible,
civil disobedience is never justified. But this is surely false,
for there are also the questions of probability and time. If
the wrong is at all a serious one, the remote (in either sense)
possibility of change is not enough reason for denying the
justified use of civil disobedience. It was Harold Laski who
pointed out the absurdity of claiming that "the duty of a
minority whose values are denied is the simple one of be-
coming a majority." The existence of alternative methods of
reform is relevant to the justification of civil disobedience,
but by no means to the extent of removing its possibility.

5. *Conscientiousness and evidence.* Whether what one   13
takes to be wrong is indeed wrong, whether innocent bystanders are likely to be hurt, whether the community will
respond to the moral claims being made, whether alternative
methods of reform are likely to be successful, these and other similar questions are susceptible to a great deal of reflection and investigation. When we act, we can only act on the
basis of what we think to be right; but recall that we can
take fewer or greater pains to determine whether what we
think to be the case is indeed so. For each degree of gravity
of an undertaking there is a degree of conscientiousness that
is appropriate. It would be silly to require a full-length
study of possible consequences to help us to decide whether
we ought to *eat out* or stay at home. But civil disobedience is
a serious business: it goes counter to the general obligation
to obey the law and almost always there are serious dangers
of undesirable consequences for others. There is, therefore,
a particular obligation to act conscientiously: to reflect
carefully about all the considerations relevant and to bring
oneself into possession of the best possible evidence pertain-

ing to the many claims that are involved in *any* act of civil disobedience.

There is no doubt in my mind that many actual cases of civil disobedience, past and present, were justified. The injustice of the laws protested against was great; the motives of those engaged in the civil disobedience were as free of self-regarding admixtures as is possible among men; the various consequences that may follow from publicly breaking the law in protest were thought about and taken into consideration; alternative methods of reform were considered and found wanting. But above all, what distinguishes such men as Thoreau and Gandhi is the thoughtful way in which they reflected about the nature and ramifications of their acts. It is sometimes forgotten that one is justified in doing what one thinks is right only to the degree to which one is conscientious in trying to determine what is right. And because of the complexity of the act and the gravity of its consequences, this last consideration is of particular importance in justifying civil disobedience.

14

Before reading section 3 of this chapter, answer the following questions.[2] These questions require you to have read the essay very carefully and they require some thought. The paragraphs in Weingartner's article have been numbered to facilitate discussion.

  (1) What is the main thesis of the essay?
  (2) How is "civil disobedience" defined and what kind of definition is given? Is the definition acceptable?
  (3) What is Weingartner's argument in paragraph four of section I for saying that civil disobedience must be non-violent? Is the argument sound?

---

2. In order to break the essay up into shorter parts so that it is easier to apply the techniques of critical reasoning to it, the reader might take questions (3), (7), (8), or (9) in isolation. Consider question (3). It is useful to write a two to three-page essay on this question. First identify Weingartner's premises. Then in your essay express the argument in standard form. Now is the argument logically correct? If it is, then consider the truth or falsity of the premises. Are any of the premises ambiguous? If you think a premise is false, then present an argument for why it is false. The same type of assignment can be given for (7), (8), or (9).

(4) According to Weingartner what is the main difference between civil disobedience and rebellion or revolution?

(5) Must a person who commits an act of civil disobedience be willing to accept the punishment for his act?

(6) In paragraph eight of section I what does Weingartner mean by "public"?

(7) In paragraph two of section II what is the argument intended to show that civil disobedience is never justified? What is Weingartner's reply? Is he correct?

(8) What is the argument in paragraph nine of section II that is meant to show this same conclusion? Is the argument sound?

(9) In paragraph ten what is the argument meant to show that civil disobedience is justified whenever the law conflicts with one's convictions? What is Weingartner's reply and is he correct?

(10) According to Weingartner, what conditions are relevant when considering whether an act of civil disobedience is justified? Is he correct?

(11) What does he mean by "the purity and strength of the motive"?

(12) What does he mean by "conscientiousness"?

5-3 Discussion of the Example

Weingartner discusses two main questions in this article:

1. What is civil disobedience?
2. Can civil disobedience be morally justified?

He defines civil disobedience as "an illegal, non-violent, moral, and public protest against a law or governmental measure." The main thesis of the essay is that there are a number of considerations that are relevant to whether an act of civil disobedience is morally justified, and each case of civil disobedience must be individually assessed on the basis of these considerations. Weingartner rejects the position that all acts of civil disobedience are wrong. He also rejects the position that as long as a law conflicts with one's moral convictions, civilly disobeying that law is justified.

There is some disagreement as to what constitutes civil disobedience. Thus it is not clear whether Weingartner's definition is intended as a report of the ordinary sense of the expression or whether it is an attempt to make the ordinary sense more precise. The definition to be found in the dictionary is not as precise as the one Weingartner offers, so it may be best to view his definition not as a reportive but as a reconstructive definition. Since a reconstructive definition is intended to make the customary sense of a term more precise, it must conform to the basic meaning of the term. Does Weingartner's definition satisfy this requirement?

In paragraph three of section I Weingartner argues that civil disobedience involves violating a law or governmental measure and hence is illegal. Most authors agree with Weingartner on this point.[3] Civil disobedience entails disobeying a law or governmental policy. If there is no violation of a law or governmental policy, then there is no *disobedience.*

Must an act of civil disobedience also be nonviolent? In paragraph four Weingartner argues that it must. His argument in standard form is:

> (1) If a person disobeys the law violently, the violence is implicitly directed against those charged with enforcing the law.
>
> (2) If it is implicitly directed against those charged with enforcing the law, then the act is not simply the transgression of a particular law; instead it is a defiance of the authority that makes and enforces the laws.
>
> (3) If it is a defiance of the authority that makes and enforces the laws, then it is not civil disobedience; instead it is rebellion.
>
> ---
>
> ∴ (4) If a person disobeys the law violently, then it is not civil disobedience; instead it is rebellion.

According to Weingartner, "Violent disobedience is not simply a noisier kind of civil disobedience; it is rebellion."

Notice that in order to put the argument into standard form we

---

3. See Hugo Adam Bedau, ed., *Civil Disobedience: Theory and Practice* (New York: Pegasus, 1969), pp. 218-19; Jeffrie G. Murphy, ed., *Civil Disobedience and Violence* (Belmont, Calif.: Wadsworth, 1971), pp. 1-5; and Robert T. Hall, *The Morality of Civil Disobedience* (New York: Harper and Row, 1971), pp. 13-17.

had to slightly rewrite some of the premises. This is very common when dealing with argumentative essays. When we reconstruct an argument either by rewriting the premises or conclusion, or by making explicit unstated premises, or by deleting superfluous material, we have to be careful not to distort the author's original argument. Having put the above argument into standard form, we are now ready to begin to critically evaluate it. First is the argument logically correct, that is, deductively valid or inductively strong? If we let the antecedents and consequents of (1) through (4) be abbreviated by the letters A, B, C, and D respectively, then the argument is:

> (1) If A, then B.
> (2) If B, then C.
> (3) If C, then D.

$\therefore$ (4) If A, then D.

Since (4) follows from the premises by two applications of hypothetical syllogism, the argument is valid.

The next question to be asked is, "Are the premises true?" In order to evaluate the truth of the premises we must of course understand what a rebellion or revolution is. According to Weingartner, in paragraph five, "Rebellion or revolution, whether it is peaceful or violent, aims to modify the established order either by supplanting those who make and enforce the laws, or by changing the very processes of legislation and enforcement, or by doing both. The change sought is not simply a change in one or another law, but of the entire framework within which laws are made and carried out." In short what distinguishes rebellion and revolution from civil disobedience is the intended goal.[4] The civil disobedient objects to particular laws or policies of the government but in general has fidelity to the system as a whole. The revolutionary does not share this fidelity. Notice that the concepts of rebellion, revolution, and civil disobedience are vague. For example, suppose a person objects to a *large* number of our laws. Does the person

---

4. Weingartner does not discuss the difference between rebellion and revolution, and for our purposes it is not necessary to do so. For a discussion of the differences see Hall, *The Morality of Civil Disobedience*, pp. 20-21, and Eugene Kamenka, "The Concept of Political Revolution," in *Philosophy For a New Generation*, edited by A. K. Bierman and James A. Gould (New York: Macmillan, 1970), pp. 380-89.

have fidelity to the system or not? In part this depends upon *which* laws he opposes. If the person is opposed to large segments of the Constitution, then we may want to say that he opposes the system as a whole. But there will be cases where it is not clear what we should say.

To assess the truth of the premises of the above argument, let us consider the following example. Suppose that the late Martin Luther King, Jr., while protesting the segregation laws in the South, had entered a restaurant for whites and had started smashing the dishes on the floor. Would it be true that his violence was implicitly directed against those charged with enforcing the law? The difficulty here is that it is not clear what Weingartner means by "implicitly directed against those charged with enforcing the law." If in our above example a policeman came to arrest King and he had thrown the dishes at the policeman, then it might be true that violence was directed against those charged with enforcing the law. But what does it mean to say that violence is *implicitly* directed against those charged with enforcing the law?

Premise (2) might help clarify premise (1). According to premise (2), King's action would not simply be the transgression of a particular law; instead it would be defiance of the authority that makes and enforces the laws. Perhaps what Weingartner means by premise (1) is something like this: if a person disobeys the law violently, although the violence may be directed at private citizens, it is also an act of defying those who enforce the law. The reasoning behind premise (2) then would be that since those who enforce the laws represent the state, it is defiance of the state, that is, it is defiance of the authority that makes and enforces the law.

With this clarification we might be willing to accept premise (1) as true. If a father orders his son to stay in the house and the son runs out slamming the door violently, the son has defied the father. If we view the father as the enforcer of certain parental regulations, then the son has defied the enforcer of those regulations. In the same sense King would have defied those charged with enforcing the laws. But does it follow that he is also defying the *authority* that makes and enforces the laws? King might very well accept the authority of the state to make and enforce laws. What he is doing is protesting a particular law. In the same way a son might recognize the parental authority of his father and yet object to a particular command. The most that can be said is that King has defied the authority of the state *in this particular case.*

He recognized the general authority of the state but defied its authority in this particular case. Premise (2) thus seems false.

Premise (3) also appears to be false. Suppose that a young man during the Vietnam war refused induction. He took his induction papers, crumbled them up, angrily threw them in the face of the induction officer, and yelled, "You have no authority to make me fight in a war that is immoral." The young man may be defying the authority of the state. But it does not follow that he is trying "to modify the established order either by supplanting those who make and enforce the laws, or by changing the very processes of legislation and enforcement, or by doing both." He may very well have fidelity to the system as a whole.

If we accepted Weingartner's argument, it seems we would also have to accept the following argument:

> (1') If a person disobeys the law, his act is implicitly directed against those charged with enforcing the law.
>
> (2') If it is implicitly directed against those charged with enforcing the law, then the act is not simply the transgression of a particular law; instead it is a defiance of the authority that makes and enforces the laws.
>
> (3') If it is a defiance of the authority that makes and enforces the laws, then it is not civil disobedience; instead it is rebellion.
>
> ---
>
> ∴ (4') If a person disobeys the law, then it is not civil disobedience; instead it is rebellion.

The same reasoning that would support (1) through (3) and hence (4) also would support (1') through (3') and hence (4'). In clarifying (1) we said that it meant that if a person disobeys the law violently, although the violence may be directed at private citizens, it is also an act of defying those who enforce the laws. If King's smashing the plates is an act of defying those who enforce the laws, then why would his illegal but nonviolent act not be an act of defying those who enforce the laws? If the son runs out of the house and does not violently slam the door, he still defies his father. Whether the act was violent makes little difference as to whether it was an act of defying those in authority. Hence if we accept (1) through (3), we must also accept (1′) through (3′). But then we are committed to the conclusion that there is no such thing as civil disobedience. Since (4′) is obviously false, we must reject Weingartner's argument. Weingartner has thus not shown that violent disobedience is rebellion or revolution, and hence he has not shown that civil disobedience must be nonviolent.

A number of philosophers have argued that civil disobedience must be nonviolent by pointing out that "civil" just means nonviolent. If one civilly disobeys the law, then by the definition of "civil" it must be nonviolent. Weingartner also seems to be appealing to this argument in the first two sentences of paragraph four. However the word "civil" is ambiguous. In one sense of the term, it refers to nonviolent behavior. Thus if one acts in a civil manner, one acts nonviolently. But in another sense of the term, it refers to the civil authorities. In this sense of "civil," if one engages in civil disobedience, one disobeys the civil authorities but it does not follow that the action must be nonviolent. The manner of disobeying the law is left unspecified. As the term "civil disobedience" was first used, it had to do with disobeying the civil authorities. In Henry David Thoreau's classic essay "On the Duty of Civil Disobedience," he defends the citizen's right to disobey the civil authorities if the individual's conscience requires him to do so. But the manner of disobeying the law—violently or nonviolently—is left open.[5] Since the word "civil" is ambiguous, it cannot be shown that civil disobedience must be nonviolent simply by appealing to the meaning of "civil."

Furthermore there is reason for not defining civil disobedience as being nonviolent. Let us return to our hypothetical story about Martin Luther King, Jr., only now imagine two cases, one where King smashes the dishes and one where he does not. The only difference in the two cases is the smashing of the dishes. The mere fact that he smashed some dishes and thus acted in a violent manner does not seem sufficient to justify excluding this as a case of civil disobedience. What is important is that he was conscientiously protesting a law that he thought was very wrong, and he was trying to make the state change the law. This is not to say that the question of violence is not important when considering acts of civil disobedience. However the question is important for deter-

---

5. The essay also was published under the title "Resistance to Civil Government." See Murphy, *Civil Disobedience and Violence*, pp. 19-38.

mining if the action was morally justified, not for determining if it was a case of civil disobedience. If a law is disobeyed violently, it becomes more difficult to justify the action. Thus when considering whether civil disobedience is *justified*, we must consider whether the act involves violence. But the mere fact that the law was disobeyed violently does not seem sufficient to conclude that the action was not an instance of civil disobedience.

When Weingartner distinguishes civil disobedience and rebellion, he says, "An important though not infallible symbol of this distinction is that in the clearest cases of civil disobedience those engaged in it are willing to accept the punishment that is meted out to those who break the law in question." Now it is not exactly clear what Weingartner means by "an important though not infallible symbol of this distinction." Perhaps he means that whether the person is willing to accept punishment is a fairly reliable indication of whether the act is a case of civil disobedience or rebellion.[6] The reasoning behind this might be as follows:

(1)   If a person illegally protests a law and is willing to accept punishment for his act, then it is probable that the person has fidelity to the system as a whole.

(2)   If it is probable that the person has fidelity to the system as a whole, then it is probable that his illegal protest is a case of civil disobedience.

∴ (3)   If a person illegally protests a law and is willing to accept punishment for his act, then it is probable that his illegal protest is a case of civil disobedience.

(1′)   If a person illegally protests a law and is not willing to accept punishment for his act, then it is probable that the person does not have fidelity to the system as a whole.

(2′)   If it is probable that the person does not have fidelity to the system as a whole, then

6. In the last sentence of paragraph six he speaks of the willingness to accept punishment as a *useful sign* that the act was a case of civil disobedience.

> it is probable that it is not a case of civil
> disobedience.

∴ (3')   If a person illegally protests a law and is not
willing to accept punishment for his act,
then it is probable that it is not a case of
civil disobedience.

To support (1) and (1') we would have to appeal to inductive
generalizations. We would have to show that most people who
illegally protest a law and who are willing to accept the punishment have fidelity to the system, while most people who are not
willing to accept the punishment do not have such fidelity. At
present we do not have sufficient data to make this generalization.
To do so would be to commit the fallacy of insufficient sample
size. At best then the willingness to accept punishment *might* be a
useful sign. It has not been shown that it is.

Some philosophers argue that in order for an act to be civil
disobedience the agent must be willing to accept the punishment.[7]
But suppose a law is clearly very unjust and the punishment for
violating it is severe. Imagine a person illegally protests this law.
Why, in order for his act to be a case of civil disobedience, must he
be willing to accept the punishment? It does not follow from the
fact that he is not willing to accept it that he does not have
fidelity to the system as a whole, hence it does not follow that his
act is not a case of civil disobedience. Other philosophers have
argued that in order for an act to be civil disobedience the agent
does not have to be willing to accept punishment; however, if an
act of civil disobedience is to be *justified,* then the agent must be
willing to accept the punishment.[8] But this is questionable also.
Why, if a law is very wrong and the punishment is severe, must a
person be willing to accept the punishment in order for his protest
to be justified? This seems just to compound the original injustice.

In paragraphs six through seven Weingartner argues that what
basically distinguishes an act of civil disobedience from an ordinary criminal action is that the former is done from a moral point

---

7. John Rawls, "The Justification of Civil Disobedience," in Bedau, *Civil Disobedience,* p. 247.

8. Sidney Hook, "Social Protest and Civil Disobedience," in Murphy, *Civil Disobedience and Violence,* p. 57.

of view. The agent believes that a law or governmental policy is morally wrong, and he commits the illegal act primarily because of this belief. The ordinary criminal can be viewed as acting primarily to gain some benefit for himself at the expense of others. His act is not done from a moral point of view but is done primarily out of self-interest. Thus if an act is to be a case of civil disobedience, it must be done from a moral point of view. Again there is general agreement with Weingartner on this point.

So far we have said that civil disobedience must be illegal and done from a moral point of view. But we have rejected the requirement that it also must be nonviolent. Can we thus define civil disobedience as an illegal act done from a moral point of view? Several authors have recently defined civil disobedience this way.[9] But such a definition must be rejected. Suppose a doctor illegally performs an abortion because he believes that the abortion law is wrong. He performs an illegal act done from a moral point of view. Should this be called a case of civil disobedience? According to Weingartner, in order for an illegal act to be civil disobedience, it must be *public*. Now what does he mean by "public"? In order for an act to be public, the agent must not conceal or attempt to conceal his action. But simply not concealing the action is not enough. The agent also must intend for his action to be known publicly. The reason for requiring the act to be public is that historically we have viewed civil disobedience as a *public protest.* One publicly makes known his disagreement with a law or some governmental policy in the hope of getting the law or policy changed. In Weingartner's terms "Simple evasion of the law, even when undertaken for the highest reasons of conscience, is not yet civil disobedience." The illegal act also must be a public protest.[10]

We can thus define civil disobedience as an illegal and public protest against a law or governmental measure where the illegal act is done from a moral point of view.[11]

In section II Weingartner examines two views on the justification

---

9. See Hall, *The Morality of Civil Disobedience*, p. 15, and Murphy, *Civil Disobedience and Violence*, p. 5.

10. There are still some unanswered questions. For example, is it sufficient for the agent to *intend* for his action to be known publicly or must he actually make his action known publicly, and what should be done to make an action known publicly?

11. In the last two paragraphs of section I, Weingartner distinguishes direct and indirect civil disobedience. This distinction does not affect the above definition.

of civil disobedience. These two views, stated in paragraph one, are:

(A)   Civil disobedience is never morally justified.
(B)   Civil disobedience is morally justified whenever it is directed against laws that conflict with one's convictions.

In paragraphs two through nine he considers the first position. Three main arguments in support of this position are critically evaluated. The first argument is considered in paragraphs two through three, the second argument in paragraphs four through eight, and the last argument in paragraph nine. Only the first and third of these arguments will be discussed here.

The first argument intended to show that civil disobedience is never justified is:

(1)   Morality consists in obedience to the laws.
(2)   If morality consists in obedience to the laws, then civil disobedience, which involves violating a law, is never morally justified.

∴ (3)   Civil disobedience is never morally justified.

The argument is valid since it is an instance of affirming the antecedent. But are the premises true? To show that premise (1) is false, Weingartner argues that it entails a number of statements that are false or certainly questionable. Suppose that at some time t there is a law that prohibits the killing of healthy innocent children, and one minute later a new law is made that makes it legal to kill such children. If premise (1) were true, then the killing of such a child at t would be wrong while a minute later it would be right. This conflicts with our ethical reasoning. The same action is not right one second and wrong the next. Also if there were conflicting laws at the same time, (1) would entail that the same action was both right and wrong. This again conflicts with our ethical reasoning. Furthermore some actions clearly seem to be morally right or wrong even though there are no laws pertaining to the action. These considerations, as well as others, provide us with sufficient reason to reject premise (1).

Another argument meant to show that no act of civil disobedience is justified rests on the claim that the consequences of such an act are disastrous. One version of the argument is:

>   (1)   If everyone practiced civil disobedience, there would be a general breakdown of the law and this would have disastrous social consequences.
> ∴ (2)   No one ought to civilly disobey the law.
>   (3)   If no one ought to civilly disobey the law, then civil disobedience is never morally justified.
> ---
> ∴ (4)   Civil disobedience is never morally justified.

Is this argument sound? As it stands it is not valid. Consider the inference from (1) to (2). It has the form:

>   (1a)   If everyone did x, it would have disastrous social consequences.
> ---
> ∴ (2a)   No one ought to do x.

Now (2a) does not follow from (1a). There are counterexamples which show that this inference is not valid. An argument that has the same form with a true premise and a false conclusion is:

>   (1b)   If everyone became a professional philosopher, it would have disastrous social consequences.
> ---
> ∴ (2b)   No one ought to become a professional philosopher.

If everyone became a professional philosopher so that there were no plumbers, electricians, builders, factory workers, maintenance engineers, and mechanics, it would have disastrous consequences. But it certainly is false that no one ought to become a professional philosopher. Thus the inference from (1) to (2) in our original argument is not valid, nor is it inductively strong. But even if the argument were valid or inductively strong, premise (1) is dubious. If everyone disobeyed the law, then a general collapse of law and order might result. But suppose that everyone publicly disobeyed a law only when they sincerely believed that the law was wrong. It is not at all clear that a lawless society would result. Premise (1) refers to everyone practicing civil disobedience, that is, to everyone illegally and publicly protesting a law from a moral point of view, not to everyone simply disobeying the law. Thus there is reason to doubt that if everyone practiced civil disobedience, the social consequences would be disastrous.

Weingartner now evaluates the thesis that civil disobedience is justified whenever one thinks the law is wrong. The argument in support of this is:

> (1) A law ought to be obeyed only if it is morally correct.
> (2) If a law ought to be obeyed only if it is morally correct, then if a person judges that a law is wrong, he is justified in disobeying it.
>
> ---
>
> ∴ (3) If a person judges that a law is wrong, he is justified in disobeying it.

Weingartner attacks (3) directly. He argues that it does not follow simply from the fact that one believes a law is wrong that one is justified in disobeying that law. If the agent's belief that the law is wrong is completely unfounded, then his disobedience is not justified. We have to consider whether the judgment was made in a conscientious way. Suppose then that we modify the argument so that the conclusion is:

> (3') If a person conscientiously judges that a law is wrong, he is justified in disobeying it.

Weingartner argues that (3') is also false. Even if a person conscientiously judges that a law is wrong, it does not follow that he is justified in disobeying it. For example, suppose a law is only slightly unfair but disobeying it would result in great suffering. In this situation, one would not be justified in disobeying the law. Even if one conscientiously judges that a law is wrong, there are other relevant considerations that must be taken into account before one would be justified in disobeying the law. Thus (3') is false.

Furthermore (1) is false. Suppose a law is wrong. Given (1) it would follow that it is not the case that we ought to obey it, that it is morally permissible not to obey it. But it may be that there are other relevant considerations that make it our duty to follow it. For example if breaking the law would produce great suffering, then it might be our duty not to break it.

Weingartner thus rejects the extreme views that civil disobedience is never justified and civil disobedience is justified whenever one judges the law is wrong. According to Weingartner there are a number of considerations that are relevant to whether an act of civil disobedience is justified, and each case of civil disobedience must be individually assessed on the basis of these considerations. In section III of the essay he discusses what these considerations are. Our discussion of this section will be brief since what Weingartner says here is basically correct. In part we will be clarifying and expanding some of his points.

The first consideration Weingartner discusses deals with the wrongness of the law. In general the greater the wrongness of the law, the greater the possibility of justifying civil disobedience. Segregation laws are gravely unjust since they violate our basic rights as human beings. In this case civil disobedience is more justifiable. On the other hand if a law is only slightly unjust, its wrongness does not override our general obligation to obey the law. For example it might be argued that our tax system is somewhat unjust. But this injustice seems not to be grievous enough to override our obligation to pay our taxes.

We also have to consider how wrong the law is *thought* to be. Since civil disobedience is done from a moral point of view, if the agent does not think the law is wrong, then it is not civil disobedience. In general the greater the law is *thought* to be wrong, the greater the possibility of justifying civil disobedience. When we consider the relationship of the law's being wrong and its being thought to be wrong, some interesting questions arise. Suppose that the law is very wrong and it is also thought to be very wrong. In this case civil disobedience would be more readily justifiable. But what happens if the law is not that grievous, only that it is thought to be very unfair? Or imagine that the law is not at all unfair, only it is thought to be. The question of conscientiousness and evidence is important here.

A second consideration has to do with the purity and strength of the motive. A person may have a number of reasons for committing an act of civil disobedience. If his act is to be civil disobedience, he must of course believe that the law is wrong. But he also may realize that if the law is changed it will directly benefit him. He may disobey the law for both of these reasons. In this case Weingartner would say that the agent has a "mixed motive." His motive is in part moral, since he believes the law is wrong and ought to be changed, but it is also in part self-regarding, since he believes that changing the law will directly benefit him. Weingartner maintains that the purer and stronger the motive for changing a law that is thought to be wrong, the greater the possibility of justifying civil disobedience. It is not exactly clear what Weingartner means by the "strength of a motive." What he seems to mean is the intensity with which one believes that the law is wrong and needs to be changed. If Jones intensely believes that a certain law is wrong and needs to be changed whereas Smith only mildly believes this, then Jones would be said to have a stronger motive for changing the law than Smith.

An extremely complex consideration pertains to the foreseeable consequences of disobeying the law. If we commit an act of civil disobedience, what is likely to happen as a result of our action? For example, suppose that we are planning to illegally hold a mass rally to protest discriminatory policies of the government. One important question is whether, as a result of holding the mass rally, there will be a confrontation with the police and violence will ensue. If it is probable that such a confrontation will occur, it becomes more difficult to justify the act of civil disobedience. Again if it is probable on the basis of the available evidence that innocent bystanders would be hurt as a result of the rally, it becomes even more difficult to justify the act. Since civil disobedience also can be violent, according to our definition, another important consideration is whether the law will be disobeyed in a violent way. We have to distinguish whether the act itself involves violence from whether, as a result of the act, violence occurs. If the illegal act is violent, the burden of justifying it becomes great.[12]

---

12. For a good discussion of the justification of violence see Robert Audi, "On the Meaning and Justification of Violence," in *Violence,* edited by Jerome A. Shaffer (New York: David McKay, 1971).

The fourth consideration that Weingartner discusses is the legal methods of reform. Some people have argued that in order for an act of civil disobedience to be justified, the legal methods of reform must first be exhausted. The difficulty with this suggestion is that it is not clear when such methods are exhausted. Furthermore, as Weingartner notes, one has to consider the time it would take for the desired change through these legal methods of reform and the likelihood of success. The strongest claim that can reasonably be made is that in a constitutional democracy such as ours, one has a general obligation to attempt to change the law through legal methods of reform first. Even this general obligation can be overriden by such considerations as the wrongness of the law, the time it would take to change the law, and the probability of getting the law changed through legal methods of reform.

Perhaps the most important consideration of all has to do with whether the act is conscientious and whether the agent's beliefs about the act are rationally justified. Since civil disobedience is such a serious affair, we are obligated to act conscientiously. For any act of civil disobedience, there are a number of important questions that must be asked. For example, is the particular law in question wrong, how wrong is it, will violence occur as a result of disobeying it, will innocent bystanders be hurt, and so on. In order for an act of civil disobedience to be conscientious at least two conditions must be satisfied. First, the agent must carefully gather the available evidence that is relevant to these questions. Second, the agent must carefully assess this evidence to determine the answers to these questions. As Weingartner notes, "one is justified in doing what one thinks is right only to the degree to which one is conscientious in trying to determine what is right." Furthermore, one is justified in doing what one thinks is right only to the degree to which the available evidence rationally justifies this belief. A person may gather and assess certain evidence and come to think that a particular law is very wrong, that disobeying it will not result in innocent bystanders being hurt, and so on. Nevertheless that evidence may not support or rationally justify these beliefs. An act of civil disobedience is morally justified only to the degree to which the agent's beliefs about the act are rationally justified by the available evidence.[13]

---

13. This last consideration is clearly illustrated in Martin Luther King, Jr., "Letter from Birmingham City Jail," in Bedau, *Civil Disobedience.*

Bibliography

For more extended discussions of the topics treated in this book, the reader will find the books in the following list useful. Copi's *Introduction to Logic,* Kahane's *Logic and Philosophy,* and the book by Carney and Scheer are general introductions to logic. They include a discussion of deductive and inductive logic as well as a discussion of topics covered in chapter 4 of this book. Kahane's *Logic and Contemporary Rhetoric* is a discussion of common fallacies. Copi's *Symbolic Logic* and the book by Kalish and Montague are excellent treatments of deductive logic. Both books include numerous examples of arguments. Pospesel's book contains five hundred deductive arguments if one desires practice in evaluating the validity of arguments. The books by Skyrms, Salmon, and Kyburg are excellent treatments of inductive logic. Besides a discussion of the basic concepts in inductive logic, they all include discussions on philosophical problems of induction. It is recommended that the reader start with the book by Skyrms as the other two are more demanding. The book by Amos, Brown, and Mink is an elementary introduction to statistics. The two books by Wallis and Roberts, and Weinberg and Schumaker are introductory treatments of statistics that require little mathematics. Huff's book is a discussion of statistical fallacies. Although the general introductions to logic mentioned above all include a discussion of topics covered in chapter 4 of this book, the books by Alston and Hospers are highly recommended.

153

Alston, William P. *Philosophy of Language.* Englewood Cliffs, N.J.: Prentice-Hall, 1964.

Amos, Jimmy R.; Brown, Foster Lloyd; and Mink, Oscar G. *Statistical Concepts: A Basic Program.* New York: Harper and Row, 1965.

Carney, James D., and Scheer, Richard K. *Fundamentals of Logic.* New York: Macmillan, 1964.

Copi, Irving M. *Introduction to Logic.* 4th ed., rev. New York: Macmillan, 1972.

———. *Symbolic Logic.* 4th ed., rev. New York: Macmillan, 1973.

Hospers, John. *An Introduction to Philosophical Analysis.* 2d ed., rev. Englewood Cliffs, N.J.: Prentice-Hall, 1967.

Huff, Darrell. *How to Lie with Statistics.* New York: W. W. Norton, 1954.

Kahane, Howard. *Logic and Contemporary Rhetoric.* Belmont, Calif.: Wadsworth, 1971.

———. *Logic and Philosophy: A Modern Introduction.* Belmont, Calif.: Wadsworth, 1969.

Kalish, Donald, and Montague, Richard. *Logic: Techniques of Formal Reasoning.* New York: Harcourt, Brace and World, 1964.

Kyburg, Henry E. *Probability and Inductive Logic.* London: Collier-Macmillan Ltd., 1970.

Pospesel, Howard. *Arguments: Deductive Logic Exercises.* Englewood Cliffs, N.J.: Prentice-Hall, 1971.

Salmon, Wesley C. *The Foundations of Scientific Inference.* Pittsburgh: University of Pittsburgh Press, 1967.

Skyrms, Brian. *Choice and Chance: An Introduction to Inductive Logic.* Belmont, Calif.: Dickenson, 1966.

Wallis, W. Allen, and Roberts, Harry V. *Statistics: A New Approach.* New York: The Free Press of Glencoe, 1956.

Weinberg, George H., and Schumaker, John A. *Statistics: An Intuitive Approach.* 2d ed. Belmont, Calif.: Brooks/Cole, 1969.

Index

155

Index   157

Refutation by logical analogy. *See* Invalidity

Requirement of total relevant information, 77-78

Sample:
  definition of, 67
  biased, 67-68 (*see also* Fallacies)
  insufficient size, 69 (*see also* Fallacies)
  random, 68
  stratified random, 68

Sentence, declarative. *See* Statement

Set of statements, consistency of. *See* Consistency

Simplification. *See* Valid argument form

Soundness of argument, 13

Statement, 1. *See also* Conditional statement; Conjunctive statement; Disjunctive statement
  simple, 23
  compound, 23

Statistical generalization. *See* Inductive generalization

Statistical syllogism, 74-82

Stratified random sample. *See* Sample

Truth:
  and inductive strength, 63
  and logical correctness, 12-14
  and validity, 19-20

Truth preserving, 20

Total relevant information. *See* Requirement of total relevant information

Universal generalization. *See* Inductive generalization

Vagueness, 101-3

Validity, deductive. *See* Deductive validity

Valid argument form:
  affirming the antecedent, 29-30
  conjunction, 26
  denying one of the disjuncts, 27
  denying the consequent, 30-31
  dilemma, 33-35
  double negation, 25
  hypothetical syllogism, 31-32
  simplification, 26